ASSURED TENANCIES

ASSURED TENANCIES

by

His Honour Judge
JAMES FOX-ANDREWS, QC
An Official Referee and a
Master of the Bench of Gray's Inn

and

DELYTH W. WILLIAMS, BA., MCD., LLB., MRTPI ACIARB
Course Director of Urban Estate Management
School of the Built Environment
Liverpool Polytechnic

1989

THE ESTATES GAZETTE LIMITED
151 WARDOUR STREET, LONDON, W1V 4BN

First Published 1989

ISBN 0 7282 0132 1

Printed in Great Britain at The Bath Press, Avon

CONTENTS

PREFACE

The Housing Act 1988 contains provisions which are intended to revolutionise the rented accommodation sector. This book is concerned only with assured tenancies, assured shorthold tenancies and assured agricultural occupancies. Whilst only some 40 sections and 4 Schedules out of some 140 sections and 18 Schedules relate to such tenancies and occupancies the provisions will signally affect many tenancies of residential dwelling-houses granted after the 14th January 1989, of which a large number will be assured. Existing tenancies will largely retain the protection they enjoyed immediately before the 1988 Act came into force on the 15th January 1989.

There are certain exceptions to this, for example on the transmission of a protected or statutory tenancy the transmitted tenancy will usually become an assured tenancy. Again on the cessation of the interest of a landlord being held by a public body or on a housing association tenancy ceasing to be such a tenancy the tenancy will in most cases become an assured one.

The major changes that the Act brings about are that a landlord may more easily obtain possession than under the Rent Act 1977 or similar legislation, that the landlord is able to obtain a market rent and that the landlord no longer has to be an approved body.

The security of tenure afforded to a tenant of an assured tenancy is different in nature and less extensive than that enjoyed under the Rent Act 1977. Nevertheless for a tenant who complies with his obligations substantial security is afforded. The fact that the landlord is entitled to receive a market rent obviously places an additional burden on the tenant. Whether this will prove socially acceptable is difficult to determine at this stage. If the Government succeed in their aim of making more rented accommodation available this may result in rent levels not rising unacceptably high. The extension of the Business Expansion Scheme to the provision of assured tenancies by the Finance Act 1988 should ensure that more houses and flats for letting do become available. Static prices for freehold houses after the recent prolonged period when values inexorably increased may assist in keeping rents at a more modest level. The extension of the BES to assured tenancies has, however, the potential for causing problems. BES companies may well be intent on getting vacant possession not later than 5 years after they have issued shares to investors. This does not appear to accord entirely with the spirit of the 1988 Act which contemplates a tenant remaining as long as he wishes but paying a market rent. High quality management would seem to be essential to ensure that tenants are selected who are willing to leave at a time convenient to the BES company.

Because of the importance of that Scheme we have included some chapters on it. It cannot be emphasised too strongly however that independent advice should always be sought before embarking on any facet of the Scheme.

Index of Abbreviations

Index of Statutes

In this book the following statutes which are frequently referred to are given the following short titles.

Landlord and Tenant Act 1954 — 1954 Act
Rent (Agriculture) Act 1976 — 1976 Act
Rent Act 1977 — 1977 Act
Housing Act 1980 — 1980 Act
Housing Act 1985 — 1985 Act
Housing and Planning Act 1986 — 1986 Act
Housing Act 1988 — 1988 Act

Other Statutes

Index of Cases

Chapter 1

Historical Background and the Future

A major objective of the Conservative Government in its third term of office has been to increase the rented accommodation market. There can be little doubt that the effect of the Rent Acts over many years particularly since the Second World War has been to throttle the availability of rented accommodation in the private sector. Compared with many parts of the Western World the private rented sector forms a tiny part of the total housing—the proportion has been assessed recently at some nine per cent.

This is a most unsatisfactory state of affairs. Mobility of labour is widely accepted as desirable. Yet without a flourishing rental sector in practice it is difficult to encourage people to move from one part of the country to another. Many people in any event for a variety of reasons wish to occupy rented accommodation rather than own their own property.

The difficulty has been to find the means whereby controls are removed or loosened without creating unacceptable social conditions.

The tinkering that took place before 1980 did little to encourage investors to provide rented accommodation. One Government's measures were almost invariably reversed by the next creating uncertainty and disillusionment among those who might otherwise have been prepared to provide additional rented accommodation.

But before 1987 the Conservative Government had placed the provision of private rented accommodation low on their agenda.

It was, however, the remarkable success of earlier legislation relating to business premises that suggested a possible solution.

By the Housing Act 1980 (hereinafter referred to as the 1980 Act) a new class of tenancy was created—the assured tenancy (a tenancy of a newly erected building)—which was subject to substantially the same rules as business tenancies under Part II of the Landlord and Tenant Act 1954 (hereinafter referred to as the 1954 Act).

But this new tenancy got off to a very hesitant start.

By April 1986 there were only six hundred such tenancies mainly in the Yorkshire and Humberside areas.

In 1986 the provisions relating to assured tenancies were extended by the Housing and Planning Act 1986 (hereinafter referred to as

1

the 1986 Act) to include dwellings where "qualifying works" had been carried out.

Only an approved body could be a landlord of an assured tenancy under the 1980 Act. The approval required was that of the Secretary of State. By this means therefore control was exercised over the identity of the landlord. In the early days a substantial number of landlords were either charities or housing associations. The most recent figure of approved bodies is about 420.

Provision was made for the situation where the landlord ceased to be an approved body.

Under the 1980 Act an assured tenancy could only be created in respect of a dwelling which was, or formed part of, a building which was erected and on which construction work first began on or after the 8th August 1980 when the Act came into force.

Further before the tenant first occupied the dwelling-house under the tenancy, no part of it could have been occupied by any person as his residence except under an assured tenancy.

Under the 1986 Act buildings already erected could be the subject of an assured tenancy so long as qualifying works had first been carried out.

Qualifying works meant works involving expenditure attributable to the dwelling-house of not less than the prescribed amount which were carried out within the period of 2 years preceding the grant of the first relevant tenancy at a time when the premises constituting the dwelling-house at the date of such grant either were not a dwelling-house or no part of them was occupied by a person as his residence. Qualifying works could be carried out before or after the date on which the 1986 Act came into force.

Provision was made for apportionment of costs where appropriate. Immediately before the coming into force of the 1988 Act the prescribed amount was £7,000 in Greater London and £5,000 elsewhere.

The dwelling-house had to be fit for human habitation at the date of the grant of the first assured tenancy. Provisions were made for an approved landlord to obtain a certification of fitness.

There were two further conditions in respect of an assured tenancy granted after qualifying works had been carried out:

(1) the dwelling-house must not have been occupied by any person as his residence except under an assured tenancy;
(2) the first assured tenancy must not have been granted to a person whether alone or jointly with others who occupied or was entitled to occupy the dwelling-house as either
    (a) a protected or statutory tenant within the meaning of

the Rent Act 1977; (hereinafter called the 1977 Act)

(b) a secured tenant within the meaning of Part IV of the Housing Act 1985 (hereinafter called the 1985 Act); or

(c) a protected occupier or statutory tenant within the meaning of the Rent (Agriculture) Act 1976 (hereinafter called the 1976 Act).

Tenancies of newly erected or improved buildings could not be assured tenancies if for example they were granted in consideration of a premium or at a low rent.

Provisions were made to tailor Part II of the 1954 Act to assured tenancies. Notices were specified for various matters.

From the landlord's point of view the significant advantage of an assured tenancy was that he could charge a market rent. The first rent was one he could freely negotiate with his tenant. The tenancy could contain rent review provisions. If a fresh tenancy was granted by the court then pursuant to Section 34 of the 1954 Act the rent would be an open market one subject only to minor limitations.

After the passing of the 1986 Act the pace of the creation of assured tenancies increased a little.

The Department of the Environment reported in October 1987 on a monitoring exercise it carried out on the scheme as at the 1st April 1987. At that time 3,674 assured tenancies were identified. The figures of a similar exercise as at 1st April 1988 are about to be published. It is expected to be about 8,000.

But in the overall context of housing this was a drop in the ocean. There was a number of reasons why the creation of assured tenancies was proceeding at such a slow rate. The requirement that the landlord should be an approved body undoubtedly proved restrictive. Although the business tenancy provisions of Part II of the 1954 Act were tailored for assured tenancies they were likely in practice to prove an ill fitting suit. Grounds for possession of a business tenancy in some respects were significantly different from those which were suitable for residential tenancies. Although as far as the authors know the provisions for the payment of compensation by a landlord to a residential tenant on the coming to an end of his tenancy in certain circumstances were never put to the test they did not appear immediately relevant.

In 1987 when the Housing Bill was launched the decision was taken to change the basis of an assured tenancy. First and foremost the landlord does not have to be an approved body. The field is now open to anyone who is able to bring himself or itself within the requirements of the 1988 Act to be a landlord of an assured tenancy. The salient features of an assured tenancy under the 1980

Act namely that an open market rental might be charged is wholly retained. But a new set of rules designed to be appropriate for a residential tenancy has been introduced. In general terms existing assured tenancies (mark 1) will become new assured tenancies (mark 2).

It is difficult to judge at this stage whether the security of tenure provisions will prove to be significantly more favourable to a landlord than was the position under the 1980 Act. Certainly as the Bill went through the House of Commons the balance was shifted a little in favour of the tenant: as originally introduced there were ten mandatory and six discretionary grounds for possession. Now there are eight of each. A tenant who discharges his obligations obtains a substantial degree of security of tenure.

It has been suggested that the provisions of Ground 2 for possession—dwelling-house subject to a mortgage granted before the beginning of the tenancy and the mortgagee wishes to exercise his right to sell it—opens up a fertile field to a landlord for obtaining possession. But this seems a little unreal to the authors. It is difficult to see why the mortgagee and the landlord will act in co-operation in such a debatable way. This is not to say that there may not be isolated cases. But *Quennel* v. *Maltby* (1978) 249 Estates Gazette 1169 (CA) may assist a tenant. So long as the tenant discharges his obligations it seems unlikely that the great majority of lenders will seek to exercise their rights.

It is an undoubted fact that after the control of rents under the Rent Acts one of the features regarded as most unsatisfactory by investors was the difficulty in obtaining possession of premises occupied by an erratic rent payer. It was only a discretionary ground for possession. It was common for courts even if persuaded to make an order for possession on this ground to suspend such orders on condition that arrears were paid off. Further the considerable costs incurred in obtaining a suspended order for possession were by no means always ordered to be paid by the tenant.

Under the Housing Bill as originally put before the House of Commons persistent delay in the payment of rent was a mandatory ground for possession. Now it is only discretionary. Only if three months arrears of rent at the date of the landlord's notice for proceedings for possession and at the date of the hearing are unpaid must a court grant an order for possession.

Under the 1980 Act, pursuant to the requirements of Part II of the 1954 Act, the initiative in taking important steps such as an application to the court for the grant of a new tenancy had to be by the tenant and had to be made within certain time limits. That is not the position under the 1988 Act.

It is certainly more logical that the mark 2 assured tenancies—which will include the mark 1 tenancies—should be subject to rules specifically designed for residential tenancies.

In general terms the protection afforded to tenancies both in respect of tenure and in respect of rent control by the 1976, 1977, 1980 and 1985 Acts will continue as regards existing tenancies or occupancies. It requires some supervening event for example the death of a tenant or a public body ceasing to hold the landlord's interests or a tenancy ceasing to be a housing association tenancy for a change to occur. Thus if someone is entitled to succeed to the tenancy held by the person who has died his tenancy thereafter will ordinarily be an assured one.

Ordinarily on the landlord's interest ceasing to be held by a public body or on a tenancy ceasing to be a housing association tenancy the tenancy will become an assured one. But save in certain cases—as to which see the chapters on "Phasing out of the Rent Act" and on "Qualifying conditions" below—many tenancies granted after the 14th January 1989 will be assured tenancies. And this is so whether the landlord is a private one or a housing association and the like.

Only in limited cases can a tenancy be granted after the 14th January 1989 attract the protection of the 1976, 1977, 1980 or 1985 Acts. For example a tenancy or licence which is entered into after the 14th January 1989 cannot be a secure tenancy unless the interest of the landlord belongs to a local authority, a new town corporation, a housing action trust established under Part III of this Act or the Development Board for Rural Wales.

Thus very large numbers of assured tenancies are likely to be created.

An additional fillip for rented accommodation was provided in the Finance Act 1988 by the extension until 31st December 1993 of the Business Expansion Scheme to the provision of assured tenancies.

It is because of this extension that in this book some consideration is given to that scheme so far as it relates to assured tenancies.

There is little doubt that the decision to extend the Business Expansion Scheme up to December 1983 to include companies specialising in the letting of residential property on the new assured tenancy basis is likely to have a substantial effect and to alter significantly the duration of many tenancies granted under that Scheme. Two-thirds of the assured tenancies under the 1980 and 1986 Acts up to the 1st April 1987 were for 21 years or more.

For landlords who look only for a rental income there will be considerable benefits in granting long leases with appropriate rent review provisions. The initial rent will be market one. Rent review provisions are likely to be index-linked or index-linked plus a percentage. Flip-flop or pendulum valuations where the valuer's task is to determine which of opposing proposals by landlord or tenant is to be preferred is again likely. Rent reviews determined by arbitrators which are appropriate for lettings of commercial properties under business tenancies where very substantial rents may be determined are unlikely to be the preferred means of determining an open market rental.

So long as tenants comply with their obligations such landlords would view it as commercially sensible that the tenant should remain paying the market rent. There would be little reason to prevent assignment. So long as the landlord retains the right to vet the proposed assignee it is economically more favourable to a landlord that the existing tenant finds a new occupier at his expense rather than that of the landlord. Only if the landlord was looking for vacant possession with a view to a profitable sale would the position be different.

But under the Business Expansion Scheme it is, at the time this book goes to print, unclear what kind and duration of assured tenancy will be granted. It seems unlikely that fixed tenancies for long terms will be granted. Whether fixed or periodical tenancies were granted it seems likely that there will be provisions for rent reviews.

A periodic tenancy may prove to have attractive features for a BES company. It can and most likely will contain rent review provisions. Although by a later amendment of section 5(1) a landlord's notice to quit is ineffective, his right to possession is protected by section 8(4)(b). If a tenant serves a notice to quit, on expiry the tenancy ceases to be assured so that section 7 does not apply. If the tenant does not vacate on due date the landlord has an immediate right to possession which he can enforce in the courts without reference to the 1988 act.

It has been suggested that under the Business Expansion Scheme fixed term tenancies for six or seven years may be granted with a prohibition against assignment and with a much enhanced rent payable from the end of the fifth year so as to encourage tenants to leave at the end of the fifth year. Whether the tenant's legal advisers will regard that as a sensible arrangement seems problematical. If as seems possible the supply and demand of rented accommodation comes more into balance a tenant will be able to be more selective.

The numerous Business Expansion Scheme prospectuses that have been issued make it clear that a very different type of tenant will be sought than is the case with other landlords. The various companies and funds identify various types of tenant who they will be seeking. Later in this book various categories are considered.

The common denominator is that these tenants will in fact only wish to be occupants for relatively short periods. Time will tell whether sufficient potential tenants of these categories exist.

It is however to be appreciated that even if £500,000,000 was invested in such schemes in a year this would produce less than ten thousand new rented dwelling-houses which is a modest number in the overall context.

The reason for this common denominator is that the landlord company will in a great majority of cases be seeking to have vacant possession of the premises if possible by the end of the fifth year so as to enable shareholders to realise their investment.

Four years is the minimum period for which the dwelling-house has to be available for letting. At the end of the fifth year any capital gains which are made will be tax free.

But assuming tenants do move after relatively short periods there may be heavy management expenses in replacing tenants: certainly a criterion for a successful BES is likely to be experienced management.

Where short tenancies are granted to persons who in the event decide they wish to stay on in occupation, BES landlords are likely to be faced with serious problems. Although numerous grounds for possession are available to a landlord the fact is that so long as the tenant complies with his obligations he is reasonably secure in his tenure. Many BES companies may in the case of some tenancies be unable to fulfil the requirements necessary to obtain possession under the available grounds.

It is difficult to judge at this stage what the political reaction to assured tenancies will be once they are widely held. If market rents increase considerably over the years it may result in calls for some kind of rent regulation, although such calls might be for a different kind of control from that which has operated in the past. If considerably more rented accommodation became available—a very possible result with BES playing a not insignificant part in this—then market rents may be held to an acceptable level.

It is the BES which may be the cause of political dissatisfaction. The likely objects of BES companies are, it seems, at odds with the overall concept of assured tenancies. It might be thought that Parliament's intention was to provide a framework in which tenants could if they wished remain for years in their rented accommodation whilst the landlords received a reasonable return on their investment. To create circumstances under which a landlord is likely to be anxious to obtain vacant possession after only a few years seems anomalous.

It is likely that the extension of the BES to assured tenancies will result in many more becoming available and this on any objective view must be to the public benefit. It may well be in practice that BES landlords and their investors will decide it prudent to defer the realisation of their assets beyond and sometimes substantially ɔeyond the five year period.

Chapter 2
Phasing Out of the Rent Act and other Transitional Provisions

General

These are very important provisions. As from 15th January 1989 in the private sector a tenancy granted pursuant to a contract made not earlier than that date will, save in exceptional circumstances, not be a protected tenancy under the 1977 Act or a relevant licence or tenancy under the 1976 Act. Under section 35 a tenancy granted by a housing association, a housing co-operative or the Housing Corporation will, save in exceptional circumstances, not be a housing association tenancy.

Only in limited cases will it be possible to grant a secure tenancy. The only landlords able to grant such a tenancy are a local authority, a new town corporation, an urban development corporation (all within the meaning of section 80 of the 1980 Act), a housing action trust established under Part III of the 1988 Act, the Development Board for Rural Works and in certain circumstances a housing co-operative.

New restricted contracts (furnished lettings) are limited by section 36 to transitional cases.

No further assured tenancies under the 1980 Act can be granted. All existing assured tenancies under that Act, save in limited cases, automatically become assured tenancies under this Act.

Section 38 deals with the position where a public body as there defined ceases to be the landlord after the 14th January 1989 of a tenancy of a dwelling-house. In general from the moment of such cessation the tenancy is not capable of being a protected tenancy, a protected occupancy or a housing association tenancy or a secure tenancy although in this limited respect it becomes a secured tenancy if the interest of the landlord becomes again held by a public body. The fact that the tenancy was entered into before or pursuant to a contract made before the 15th January 1989 does not of itself prevent it becoming an assured tenancy despite the provisions of paragraph 1 of Schedule 1 excluding such a tenancy from being or becoming an assured tenancy.

By section 39 important provisions are made in the case of protected or statutory tenancies under the 1977 Act or agricultural occupancies or statutory tenancies under the 1976 Act and in respect of such persons as are entitled to succeed. Such persons will ordinarily succeed to an assured tenancy, an assured shorthold tenancy or an assured agricultural occupancy.

It is important to appreciate that protected, secure, housing association and agricultural tenancies entered into before, or pursuant to a contract made before, the 15th January 1989 are entirely unaffected by this Act. Unless and until some event occurs such as the death of the tenant or a public body ceasing to have the interest of the landlord the tenant will continue to enjoy the same protection as he did prior to the 15th January 1989.

New protected tenancies under the 1977 Act or agricultural occupancies restricted to special cases

Section 34 contains extensive provisions in these respects.

A protected tenancy is a contractual tenancy of a dwelling-house which attracts the full protection of the 1977 Act both as to regulation of rent and as to security of tenure.

Upon the termination of a protected tenancy of a dwelling-house a person who, immediately before that termination, was in possession as a protected tenant, if and so long as he continues to occupy it as his residence is the statutory tenant of it.

Notwithstanding that under a tenancy a dwelling-house is let as a separate dwelling the tenancy is not necessarily protected under the 1977 Act. It may or may not be subject to a different kind of protection or control.

Tenancies which are not protected tenancies are those in respect of dwelling-houses whose rateable value exceeds certain amounts, dwelling-houses let on low rents, tenancies where board or attendance is provided, agricultural holdings, tenancies where the landlord's interest is held by the Crown, student and holiday lettings, houses let with other land, lettings by public bodies, lettings by resident landlords, parsonage houses and assured tenancies under the 1980 Act.

A tenancy entered into on or after the 15th January 1989 cannot be a protected tenancy in the absence of certain limited circumstances. But in the following circumstances a tenancy entered into on or after the 15th January 1989 will still be protected. If such tenancy is entered into in pursuance of a contract made before the 15th January 1989. Again if the tenancy is granted to a person, alone or jointly with others, who immediately before the tenancy was granted was a protected or statutory tenant and is so granted by the person who at the time was the landlord, or one of the joint landlords, under the protected or statutory tenancy. But such a protected or statutory tenant does not include a tenant under a protected shorthold tenancy or a protected or statutory tenant which was let under a protected shorthold tenancy which has ended and in respect of which either there has been no grant of a further tenancy or any grant of a further tenancy has been made to the person who immediately before the grant, was in possession of the dwelling-house as a protected or statutory tenant.

A "protected shorthold tenancy" includes a tenancy which, in proceedings for possession under Case 19 in Schedule 15 to the 1977 Act, is treated as a protected shorthold tenancy.

Again where a court gives a landlord possession of a dwelling-house the subject of a protected or statutory tenancy or of an agricultural occupancy on the ground that the alternative accommodation offered by the landlord is suitable then the tenancy of such alternative accommodation may become a protected tenancy if the court considers that, in the circumstances, the grant of an assured tenancy would not afford the required security and it makes a direction that the new tenancy will be a protected one.

Finally a tenancy will be a protected one where the interest of the landlord previously held by a new town corporation ceases to be so held between the 15th November 1988 and 14th November 1990 (or such earlier or later date as may be specified). After the later date, whenever it may be, the tenancy ceases to be a protected one.

Where the circumstances above considered do not exist with the result that the tenancy is not a protected one then if the tenancy is an assured one section 34(3) provides that it shall be an assured shorthold tenancy whether or not it fulfils the conditions in section 20(1) of the 1988 Act unless, before the tenancy is entered into, the landlord serves notice on the tenant that it is not to be a shorthold tenancy.

See chapter 10 on assured shorthold tenancies.

The 1976 Act provides security of tenure for agricultural workers who had previously been licensees in respect of the tied cottages which they occupied or who had been tenants under a tenancy with a rent of less than two-thirds of the rateable value or at no rent at all.

A relevant licence is a licence of a separate dwelling-house with exclusion occupation and which if it were a tenancy would have been protected by the Rent Act but for the fact that the right to occupy was at a low rent or at no rent. A relevant tenancy is a tenancy of a dwelling-house let as a separate dwelling which would be protected by the Rent Act but for the same fact.

New housing association tenancies restricted to special cases and limitation as to the circumstances in which new secure tenancies can be granted

Section 35 contains provision in respect of these matters.

Part VI of the 1977 Act applied rent limits for dwellings let by housing associations, housing trusts and the Housing Corporation. Section 86 of that Act applied that part to a tenancy other than a co-ownership; tenancy where:

(a) the interest of the landlord under the tenancy belonged to a housing association or housing trust or to the Housing Corporation; and

(b) the tenancy would be a protected tenancy but for section 15 or 16 of that Act (landlord's interest belonging to a housing association or a housing co-operative) and is not a tenancy to which Part II of the 1954 Act (business tenancies) applies.

A secure tenancy was created by section 28 of the 1980 Act. Its present definition is that contained in section 79 of the 1985 Act. A tenancy under which a dwelling-house is let as a separate dwelling is a secure tenancy at any time when the conditions described in sections 80 and 81 of that Act as the "landlord conditions" and the "tenant conditions" are satisfied save in certain circumstances. The landlord conditions are satisfied where the interest of the landlord belongs to, amongst others, the Housing Corporation, a housing trust which is a charity and certain housing associations or housing co-operatives.

A tenancy which is entered into on or after the 15th January 1989 cannot be a housing association tenancy unless:

(a) it is entered into in pursuance of a contract made before the 15th January 1989; or

(b) it is granted to a person, alone or jointly with others, who immediately before the tenancy was granted, was a tenant under a housing association tenancy and is so granted by the person who at that time was the landlord under that housing association tenancy; or

(c) it is granted to a person, alone or jointly with others, in the following circumstances:

(i) Prior to the grant of the tenancy, an order for possession of a dwelling-house was made against him, alone or jointly with others, on the court being satisfied on the grounds set out in Part II of Schedule 2 to the 1985 Act (grounds on which a court may order possession if suitable alternative accommodation is available) or Part III (grounds on which a court may order possession if it considers it reasonable and suitable alternative accommodation is available); and

   (ii) the tenancy is of the premises which constitute the suitable alternative accommodation as to which the court was so satisfied; and

   (iii) in the proceedings for possession the court directed that the tenancy would be a housing association tenancy; or

(d) The interest of a landlord previously held by a new town corporation ceases to be so held between the 15th November 1988 and the 14th November 1990 (or such earlier or later date as may be specified). After the latter date, whenever it may be, the tenancy will cease to be a secure one.

Special provisions are made in respect of the grant of a tenancy whether before or after 15th January 1989 by a registered housing association, within the meaning of the Housing Association Act 1985 of a defective dwelling to a former owner-occupier under section 554 of the 1985 Act, pursuant to an obligation (see now new section 554(2A) introduced by para. 61 of Schedule 17 to the 1988 Act). It is to be assumed for the purposes only of section 86(2)(b) of the 1977 Act (tenancy would be a protected tenancy but for sections 15 or 16—landlord's interest belonging to a housing association or a housing co-operative) that the tenancy was granted before the 15th January 1989.

A tenancy or licence which is entered into on or after the 15th January 1989 cannot be a secure tenancy unless:

(a) the interest of the landlord belongs to a local authority, a new town corporation, or an urban development corporation, all within the meaning of section 80 of the 1985 Act, a housing action trust established under Part III of the 1988 Act or the Development Board for Rural Wales; or

(b) the interest of the landlord belongs to a housing co-operative within the meaning of section 27B of the 1985 Act (agreements between local housing authorities and housing co-operatives) and the tenancy or licence is a dwelling-house comprised in the housing co-operative agreement falling within that section; or

(c) it is entered into in pursuance of a contract made before the 15th January 1989; or

(d) it is granted to a person, alone or jointly with others, who immediately before it was entered into, was a secure tenant and is so granted by the body which at that time was the landlord or licensor under the secure tenancy; or

(e) it is granted to a person, alone or jointly with others, in the following circumstances:

   (i) Prior to the grant of the tenancy or licence, an order for possession of a dwelling-house was made against him (either alone or jointly with others) on the court being satisfied on the grounds set out in Part II of Schedule 2 to the 1985 Act (grounds on which the court may order possession if suitable alternative accommodation is available) or Part III (grounds on which a court may order possession if it considers it reasonable and suitable alternative accommodation is available); and

   (ii) the tenancy or licence is of the premises which constitute the suitable accommodation as to which the court was so satisfied; and

   (iii) in the proceedings for possession the court considered that, in the circumstances, the grant of an assured tenancy would not afford the required security and, accordingly, directed that the tenancy or licence should be a secure tenancy; or

(f) if it is granted pursuant to an obligation under section 554 (2A) of the 1985 Act as introduced by para. 61 of Schedule 17 to the 1988 Act.

Finally provision is made for the position where whilst a protected or statutory tenancy is continuing the interest of the landlord comes to be held by a housing association, a housing trust, the Housing Corporation or Housing for Wales. In such circumstances other provisions in the Act are to be disregarded and the tenancy will become a housing association tenancy or a secure tenancy as the case may be.

New restricted contracts limited to transitional cases

Section 36 contains provisions in this respect.

A restricted contract is one whereby a person grants to another the right to occupy a dwelling-house as a residence in consideration of a rent which includes payment for the use of furniture or for services but which does not create a protected or statutory tenancy. Since the Rent Act 1974 a tenancy was no longer prevented from being a protected or statutory tenancy by reason only of the fact that the rent included payment for the use of furniture.

Thus most furnished lettings which before the coming into force of that Act were unprotected became subject to the Rent Acts. The provisions of the Rent Acts were further extended to certain furnished tenancies granted by a resident landlord where the landlord remained in residence. A licensee may also obtain the same protection as a tenant but he must have exclusive occupation of at least some part of the dwelling-house.

Section 36(1) provides that a tenancy or other contract entered into after the 15th January 1989 cannot be a restricted contract for the purposes of the 1977 Act unless it is entered into in pursuance of a contract made before the 15th January 1989.

Provision is made for the situation where a restricted contract was entered into before or pursuant to a contract made before the 15th January 1989 but was varied thereafter.

But that provision is subject to a number of qualifications. A variation effecting the amount of rent does not include a reference to a reduction or increase of rent by a rent tribunal under section 78 of the 1977 Act. And it does not include a reference to a variation which is made by the parties and has the effect of making the rent expressed to be payable under the contract the same as the rent for the dwelling which is entered in the register under section 79 of the 1977 Act.

Sub-section (1) of section 81A of the 1977 Act introduced by the 1980 Act which relates to the requirement that a rent tribunal shall cancel a registration of rent in certain circumstances ceases to have effect on 15th January 1989.

Transfer of Mark 1 assured tenancies to assured tenancies under the Housing Act 1988

'Mark 1' assured tenancies are still of importance due to the operation of sections 1(3),(4) and 37 of the 1988 Act. Under the provisions of section 1(3) of the 1988 Act a tenancy under which a dwelling-house was let as a separate dwelling and which immediately before the commencement of the 1988 Act was an assured tenancy under the 1980 Act becomes an assured tenancy under the 1988 Act. In the case of these converted "old style" assured tenancies only the exclusions relating to Crown tenancies and local authority and public tenancies in paras 11 and 12 of Schedule I to the 1988 Act apply and none of the other exclusions in that

Schedule. Thereafter sections 56 to 58 of Schedule 5 to the 1980 Act cease to apply to such a converted tenancy.

Section 37(1) provides that a tenancy entered into on or after the 15th January 1989 cannot be an assured tenancy for the purposes of the 1980 Act. The following is a suggested analysis of the various possibilities concerning the transfer of 'Mark 1' assured tenancies to the new scheme of the 1988 Act:

(a) A tenancy which immediately before the 15th January 1989 was an assured tenancy under the 1980 Act becomes an assured tenancy under the 1988 Act; section 1(3)(a),(b). In such a case Part I of Schedule I has effect as if it consisted only of paragraphs 11 (Crown tenancies) and 12 (local authority tenancies).

(b) A tenancy entered into on or after the commencement of the 1988 Act cannot be an assured tenancy for the purposes of the 1980 Act; section 37(1).

(c) Where a tenant under the 1980 Act made an application to the court, under section 24 of the 1954 Act, for the grant of a new tenancy before the 15th January 1989 and the application was continuing on the 15th January 1989, such a tenancy is not converted into an assured tenancy under the 1988 Act; section 37(2).

(d) If, in the circumstances outlined in (c) (above), the court makes an order under section 29 of the 1954 Act that tenancy is an assured tenancy under the 1988 Act: section 37(3).

(e) Where a contract was entered into for the grant of an assured tenancy under the 1980 Act before the 15th January 1989 but at that date the tenancy had not been granted the contract is deemed to be a contract for the grant of an assured tenancy within the 1988 Act: section 37(4)(a),(b).

It is to be noted that in the case of (d) and (e) (above) Part I of Schedule I to the 1988 Act (which defines those tenancies which cannot be assured tenancies) has effect as if the only excluded tenancies were those contained in paragraphs 11 and 12 (Crown tenancies and local authority tenancies etc respectively).

Transfer of existing tenancies from the public to the private sector

Section 38 makes provision for the position where the interest of a landlord under a tenancy is held by a public body at a time when:

(a) it belongs to a local authority, a new town corporation or an urban development corporation, all within the meaning of section 80 of the 1985 Act; or

(b) belongs to a housing action trust (this is a corporation created by the 1988 Act and is dealt with in sections 60–92 of the Act); or

(c) it belongs to the Development Board for Rural Wales; or

(d) it belongs to Her Majesty in right of the Crown or to a government department or is held in trust for Her Majesty for the purpose of a government department.

Provision is also made for a housing association tenancy which ceases to be of that nature.

Where a tenancy is entered into before, or pursuant to a contract made before, the 15th January 1989 then if on the 15th January, or if it is later, at the time it is entered into, the interest of the landlord is a public body or the tenancy is a housing association tenancy and either the interest of the landlord ceases to be held by a public body or the tenancy ceases to be a housing association tenancy then certain consequences ensue.

From that time the tenancy is not capable of being a protected tenancy, a protected occupancy or a housing association tenancy.

The tenancy is not capable of being a secure tenancy unless (and only at a time when) the interest of the landlord is (or is again) held by a public body. The provisions of paragraph 1 of Part I of Schedule 1 to the 1988 Act which provide that a tenancy which is entered into before, or pursuant to a contract made before, the 15th January 1989 cannot be an assured tenancy are of no effect. Whether or not in such circumstances the tenancy becomes or remains an assured tenancy depends on whether the Qualifying Conditions are satisfied as to which see chapter 3 below.

Special provision is made in respect of tenancies where the interest of a landlord is held by a new town corporation within the meaning of section 80 of the 1985 Act.

The provisions already noted regarding tenancies where the interest of the landlord is held by a public body and housing association tenancies apply equally to tenancies where the interest of the landlord is held by a new town corporation save that instead of the 15th January 1989 being the relevant date the relevant date is the 14th November 1990 or such earlier or later date as the Secretary of State may specify by statutory instrument.

Statutory tenants: succession

Section 39 and Schedule 4 make extensive provisions in this respect.

This is dealt with fully under chapter 6—Succession. In general where a protected or statutory tenant or an agricultural occupant or statutory tenant dies the person, if any, entitled to remain will do so under an assured tenancy, an assured shorthold tenancy or an assured agricultural occupancy depending on the circumstances.

Chapter 3
Qualifying Conditions

(i) A "tenancy"

There must be a tenancy under which a dwelling-house is let as a separate dwelling so that a licence agreement cannot amount to an assured tenancy. The test to be applied in such a case is as enunciated in *Street* v. *Mountford* [1985] 1 EGLR 128 [1985] AC 809 namely that for a tenancy to arise there must be exclusive possession for a term at a rent so that if the occupier is not a lodger he must be a tenant. See also *Antoniades* v. *Villiers* (1988) 47 Estates Gazette 193.

(ii) "Dwelling-house let as a separate dwelling"

It is a question of fact whether premises are a house or not and in *Langford Property Co. Ltd.* v. *Goldrich* [1949] 1 KB 511 a house has been held to include a flat. The question of whether a dwelling-house is let as a separate dwelling was considered in *British Land Co. Ltd.* v. *Herbert Silver (Menswear) Ltd.* [1958] 1 QB 530 in the context of the Rent Act provisions where Upjohn J. was of the opinion that "... on the issue whether the premises are let as a separate dwelling you must look to the bargain made between the parties and see for what purpose the parties intended the premises would be used. If that does not provide an answer, you look to all the surrounding circumstances and see what must have been in the contemplation of the parties; if that yields no solution, you must look to the nature of the premises and the actual user at the relevant time."

In this context it is necessary to consider whether the dwelling-house is let as a separate dwelling because the tenancy can be an assured tenancy if the dwelling-house is occupied by a tenant or joint tenants (section 1(1)(a)). There are particular provisions in section 3(1) of the 1988 Act where the tenant is sharing accommodation with persons other than the landlord. Where a tenant has exclusive occupation of any accommodation (the separate accommodation) and the terms of his tenancy include the use of other accommodation in common with another person(s) (not being or including the landlord), and the sharing of such accommodation is the only reason for the tenancy's exclusion from being an assured tenancy, the separate accommodation is deemed to be held on an assured tenancy.

There are special provisions applicable to shared accommodation which are contained in section 10. Under these provisions, in any case falling within the circumstances envisaged in section 3, no order shall be made for possession of any of the shared accommodation while the tenant is in possession of the separate accommodation (whether on the application of the immediate landlord, of the tenant or any person under whom that landlord derives title) unless a like order has been made (or is made at the same time) in respect of the separate accommodation. The landlord may apply to the court to make such order as it thinks just, namely:

(a) terminating the right of the tenant to use the whole or any part of the shared accommodation other than living accommodation; or

(b) modifying his right to use the whole or any part of the shared accommodation, whether by varying the persons or increasing the number of persons entitled to the use of that accommodation or otherwise.

However, no order can be made under section 10 so as to effect any termination or modification of the rights of the tenant which, apart from section 3(3), could not be effected by or under the terms of the tenancy.

The position where the dwelling-house is let together with other land is dealt with in section 2(1)(a),(b) so that if the main purpose of the letting is the provision of a home for the tenant (or where there are joint tenants at least one of them) the "other land" is treated as part of the dwelling-house. Where the main purpose is not the provision of a home the dwelling is not treated as let as a separate dwelling. There is a further saving provision in section 4(1) whereby if a tenant of a dwelling-house has sublet part, but not the whole, of the dwelling-house then as against the landlord or any superior landlord no part of the dwelling-house is to be treated as excluded from being a dwelling-house let on an assured tenancy by reason only that the terms of the subletting include the use of accommodation in common with other persons.

The tenant, or each of the joint tenants, must be an individual so that an assured tenancy cannot be held by a company. It is clear that this provision in the 1988 Act emanates from the long-standing rule under the Rent Acts enunciated in *Skinner* v. *Geary* [1931] 2 KB 546 that the "protection which the Acts afford is to the tenant in his own home. It is a personal thing."

(iii) Occupation as only or principal home

It is clear from section 1(1)(b) that the qualifying conditions will not be met unless the dwelling-house is occupied as his only or principal home. The question of whether the test of "occupation" is satisfied is one of fact but it is submitted that a non-occupying tenant cannot satisfy the test and cannot, therefore, hold an assured tenancy. If the assured tenancy is held by joint tenants only one of the tenants is required to occupy to satisfy the condition in section 1(1)(b). It is useful to consider the decision in *Brown* v. *Brash* [1948] 2 KB 247 where it was held that the question of occupation was one of fact and degree and the question of absence from occupation could be approached as follows:

(1) the onus is on the tenant to rebut the presumption that his possession has ceased.

(2) to rebut it he must, at all events, establish a *de facto* intention on his part to return after his absence.

(3) but neither in principle nor on the authorities can this be enough. To suppose that he can absent himself for 5 or 10 years or more and retain possession and his protected status simply by proving an inward intention to return after so protracted an absence would be to frustrate the spirit and policy of the Act.

(4) notwithstanding an absence so protracted the authorities suggest that its effect may be averted if he couples and clothes his inward intention with some formal, outward, and visible sign of it, i.e. instals in the premises some caretaker or representative, be it a relative or not, with the status of a licensee and with the function of preserving the premises for his own ultimate homecoming. There will then, at all events, be someone to profit by the housing accommodation involved which will not stand empty. It may be that the same result can be secured by leaving on the premises a deliberate symbol of continued occupation such as furniture. Apart from authority, in principle possession in fact (for it is with possession in fact and not with possession in law that we are here concerned) requires not merely *"animus possidendi"* but *"corpus possessionis,"* viz., some visible state of affairs in which *animus possidendi* finds expression.

(5) if the caretaker (to use that term for short) or the furniture be removed from the premises otherwise than quite temporarily, we are of opinion that the protection, artificially prolonged by their presence, ceases, whether the tenant wills

or desires such removal or not.

In considering the question of whether a particular tenant can satisfy the test of "his only or principal home" under section 1(1)(b) regard should be had to the question of whether a person can qualify as an assured tenant if he is also occupying another dwelling-house in addition to the one held under an assured tenancy. On a similar issue under the 1977 Act the tests to be applied were outlined in *Hampstead Way Investments Ltd.* v. *Lewis-Weare* 274 Estates Gazette 281 [1985] 1 WLR 164:

(i)   a person may have two dwelling-houses, each of which he occupies as his home, so that, if either of them is let to him, his tenancy of it is protected by the 1977 Act.

(ii)   where a tenant is a tenant of two different parts of the same house under different lettings by the same landlord and carries on some of his living activities in one part of the house and the rest of them in the other part, neither tenancy would normally be protected. If, however, the true view of the facts is that there was, in substance, a single combined or composite letting of the two parts of the house as a whole, then the tenancies of both parts together will, or anyhow may, be protected.

(iii)   where a person owns one dwelling-house which he occupies as his home for most of the time, and is at the same time the tenant of another dwelling-house which he occupies rarely or for limited purposes it is a question of fact and degree whether he occupied the latter dwelling-house as his second home.

(iv) Rateable value limits

There are two rules concerning the rateable value limits, contained in section 1(2)(b) of and Schedule 1 to the 1988 Act, which are to be applied in determining whether a tenancy satisfies the requirement of an assured tenancy. Firstly, a tenancy under which the dwelling-house has a rateable value exceeding £750 (£1,500 in Greater London) is outside the 1988 Act. Secondly, a tenancy under which either no rent is payable or the rent payable is less than two-thirds of the rateable value of the dwelling-house cannot be an assured tenancy. Both these rateable value tests are applicable to the "rateable value of the dwelling-house for the time being" and there are no provisions in the 1988 Act on the determination of the rateable value limits on the "appropriate day" similar to those of the Rent Act 1977.

Greater London is an administrative area which was created by the London Government Act 1963. It comprises the London Boroughs, the City of London and the Inner and Middle Temples. It is larger than the area of the old London County Council. It does not entirely match the area of the Metropolitan Police District as it both includes and excludes parts without and within that district.

It is to be noted that there are provisions in Part II of Schedule I to the 1988 Act for ascertaining the rateable value of the dwelling-house. In the case of the dwelling-house which is a hereditament for which a rateable value is then shown on the valuation list it is that rateable value. However, if the dwelling-house forms part only of such a hereditament or consists of or forms part of more than one such hereditament, its rateable value shall be taken to be such value as is found by a proper apportionment or aggregation of the rateable value or values so shown. Any question arising as to the proper apportionment or aggregation of any value or values is to be determined by the county court; para 15(2) of Schedule I to the 1988 Act.

Exclusions from Assured Tenancies

The following tenancies cannot be assured tenancies under section 1(1)(c) of and Schedule I to the 1988 Act:

(i) Tenancies entered into before the commencement of the 1988 Act

A tenancy entered into before, or pursuant to a contract made before, the 1988 Act came into force, except, of course, most assured tenancies under the 1980 Act. In addition certain existing tenancies may become assured tenancies under section 38 where there is a transfer of the landlord's interest from the public to the private sector or where a housing association tenancy ceases to be one.

(ii) Tenancies of dwelling-houses with high rateable values

A tenancy under which the dwelling-house has for the time being a rateable value which,

    (a) if it is in Greater London, exceeds £1,500; and
    (b) if it is elsewhere, exceeds £750.

(iii) Tenancies at a low rent

A tenancy under which either no rent is payable or the rent payable
is less than two-thirds of the rateable value of the dwelling-house
for the time being cannot be an assured tenancy. In determining
whether a tenancy is a tenancy at a low rent there shall be disregarded such part (if any) of the sums payable by the tenant as is
expressed (in whatever terms) to be payable in respect of rates,
services, management, repairs, maintenance or insurance, unless it
could not have been regarded by the parties to the tenancy as a
part so payable.

It is apparent that somewhat late in the day in the passage of
the Bill through Parliament the Government considered that on a
logical basis tenancies to which Part I of the 1954 Act applied (leases
for more than 21 years at a low rent) should become assured tenancies at the end of the fixed term instead of statutory tenancies under
which tenants paid "a fair rent". The Local Government and Housing Bill 1989 seeks to deal with this.

(iv) Business tenancies under the 1954 Act

A tenancy to which Part II of the 1954 Act applies.

(v) Licensed premises

A tenancy under which the dwelling-house consists of or comprises
premises licensed for the sale of intoxicating liquors for consumption
on the premises.

(vi) Tenancies of agricultural land

A tenancy under which agricultural land, exceeding two acres, is
let together with a dwelling-house. In this context the term "agricultural land" is as defined in section 26(3)(a) of the General Rate
Act 1967.

(vii) Tenancies of agricultural holdings

A tenancy under which the dwelling-house

(a) is comprised in an agricultural holding within the meaning
     of the Agricultural Holdings Act 1986; and
(b) is occupied by the person responsible for the control
     (whether as tenant or as servant or agent of the tenant)
     of the farming of the holding.

(viii) Lettings to students

A tenancy which is granted to a person who is pursuing, or intends to pursue a course of study provided by a specified educational institution and is so granted either by that institution or by another specified institution or body of persons. This is intended to cover the situation where the institution owns the premises.

(ix) Holiday Lettings

A tenancy the purpose of which is to confer on the tenant the right to occupy the dwelling-house for a holiday.

(x) Resident landlords

A tenancy in respect of which the following conditions are fulfilled cannot be an assured tenancy where it is let by a resident landlord:

(a) that the dwelling-house forms part only of a building and, except in a case where the dwelling-house also forms part of a flat, the building is not a purpose-built block of flats; and

(b) that the tenancy was granted by an individual who, at the time when the tenancy was granted, occupied as his only or principal home another dwelling-house which,
  (i) in the case mentioned in paragraph (a) above, also forms part of the flat; or
  (ii) in any other case, also forms part of the building;

(c) that, subject to Part III of Schedule 1, at all times since the tenancy was granted the interest of the landlord under the tenancy has belonged to an individual who, at the time he owned that interest, occupied as his only or principal home another dwelling-house which,
  (i) in the case mentioned in paragraph (a) above, also formed part of the flat; or
  (ii) in any other case, also formed part of the building; and

(d) that the tenancy is not one which is excluded from this sub-paragraph by sub-paragraph (3) below.

Sub-paragraph (3) of paragraph 10 of Schedule 1 provides
"(3) A tenancy (in this sub-paragraph referred to as "the new tenancy") is excluded from sub-paragraph (1) above if—

(a) it is granted to a person (alone, or jointly with others) who, immediately before it was granted, was a tenant under an assured tenancy (in this sub-paragraph referred to as "the former tenancy") of the same dwelling-house or of another dwelling-house which forms part of the building in question; and

(b) the landlord under the new tenancy and under the former tenancy is the same person or, if either of those tenancies is or was granted by two or more persons jointly, the same person is the landlord or one of the landlords under each tenancy."

(xi) Crown tenancies

A tenancy under which the interest of the landlord belongs to the Crown or to a government department or is held in trust for the Crown for the purposes of a government department cannot be an assured tenancy. But the exclusion does not apply where the interest belongs to the Crown and is under the management of the Crown Estates Commissioners.

(xii) Local authority tenancies

A tenancy under which the interest of the landlord belongs to one of the following cannot be an assured tenancy:

(a) a local authority, namely
 (i)   the council of a county, district or London borough;
 (ii) the Common Council of the City of London;
 (iii) the Council of the Isles of Scilly;
 (iv) the Broads Authority;
 (v)   the Inner London Education Authority; and
 (vi) a joint authority, within the meaning of the Local Government Act 1985.
(b) the Commission for the New Towns;
(c) the Development Board for Rural Wales;
(d) an urban development corporation established by an order under section 135 of the Local Government, Planning and Land Act 1980;
(e) a development corporation, within the meaning of the New Towns Act 1981;
(f) an authority established under section 10 of the Local Government Act 1985 (waste disposal authorities);
(g) a residuary body, within the meaning of the Local Government Act 1985; or
(h) a fully mutual housing association, within the meaning of Part I of the Housing Associations Act 1985; or

  (i)   a housing action trust established under Part III of the 1988 Act.

(xiii) *Transitional cases*

The following existing tenancies cannot be assured tenancies:

  (a) A protected tenancy, within the meaning of the 1977 Act
  (b) A housing association tenancy, within the meaning of Part VI of the 1977 Act
  (c) A secure tenancy
  (d) Where a person is a protected occupier of a dwelling-house, within the meaning of the 1976 Act, the relevant tenancy, within the meaning of that Act, by virtue of which he occupies the dwelling-house.

(xiv) *Arrangements by a local authority*

If a local authority, acting in pursuance of its duty under sections 63, 65(3) or 68(1) of the 1985 Act, makes arrangements with another person to provide accommodation, a tenancy granted by that other person in pursuance of the arrangements to a person specified by the local authority cannot be an assured tenancy before the expiry of the period of twelve months beginning with the date on which the tenant received notice under section 64(1) or 68(3) of the 1985 Act unless (before the expiry of that period) the tenant is notified by the landlord that the tenancy is to be regarded as an assured tenancy; section 1(5),(6).

Chapter 4

Security of Tenure and Fixing of Terms of a Statutory Periodic Tenancy

It is a cardinal provision of the 1988 Act that a tenant of an assured tenancy has security of tenure unless and until a court otherwise orders. He may of course by his voluntary act bring the tenancy to an end, for example by surrender. Even if a fixed term tenancy contains powers for a landlord to determine the tenancy in certain circumstances and the landlord exercises that power an order of the court is still required before the landlord is entitled to possession.

On a fixed term tenancy coming to an end by effluxion of time the tenant is entitled to remain in possession under a statutory periodic tenancy. Such a tenancy springs into being immediately after the ending of the fixed term. It is deemed to have been granted by the person who was the landlord under the fixed tenancy immediately before it came to an end. The premises comprised in this statutory periodic tenancy are the same as those in the fixed term tenancy. The periods of a statutory periodic tenancy are the same as those for which rent was last payable under the fixed term tenancy. Save in the respects indicated below the statutory periodic tenancy is one under which the other terms are the same as those of the fixed term tenancy immediately before it came to an end, except that any term which makes provision for determination by the landlord or the tenant shall not have effect while the tenancy remains an assured tenancy.

All the terms set out in this last paragraph are called "the implied terms".

If either party wishes the terms of the statutory periodic tenancy to be different from those contained in the fixed term tenancy then not later than the first anniversary of the day on which the fixed term tenancy came to an end either party may serve on the other a notice in the prescribed form proposing terms of the statutory periodic tenancy different from the implied terms and if the landlord or the tenant considers it appropriate, proposing an adjustment of the amount of rent to take account of the proposed terms. The rent adjustment in these circumstances is of a quite different nature from the increase of rent which may take place under section 13 which is considered in chapter 5.

If either party on whom such a notice is served is content with the proposed new terms and where applicable the proposed adjustment consequent thereon he need do nothing. On the date proposed in the notice which must be a date not earlier than three months from the date the notice is served the terms proposed in the notice become terms of the tenancy in substitution for any of the implied terms dealing with the same subject-matter and the amount of the proposed rent adjustment (if any) are varied. If, however, the party on whom the notice is served is not content with the proposal he must then make an application in the prescribed form referring the notice to a rent assessment committee. That prescribed form is to be found in Appendix A.

Upon such reference the committee is required to consider the terms proposed in the notice and to determine whether those terms or some other proposed terms (dealing with the same subject-matter as the proposed terms), are such as, in its opinion, might reasonably to be found in an assured periodic tenancy of the dwelling-house concerned being a tenancy:

(a) which begins on the coming to an end of the fixed term tenancy; and

(b) which is granted by a willing landlord on terms which, except insofar as they relate to the subject-matter of the proposed terms, are those of the statutory periodic tenancy at the time of the committee's consideration.

It matters not that the notice under its consideration is silent as to a proposed adjustment of rent because the committee which determines any terms different from the implied terms is required, if it considers it appropriate, to specify such an adjustment to take account of the term so determined.

In making an adjustment whether a notice requests such an adjustment or not the committee has to disregard any effect on the terms or the amount of the rent attributable to the granting of a tenancy to a sitting tenant.

In the event of a reference to the committee by a landlord or a tenant the date of the coming into effect of terms determined by it is, unless the landlord and tenant otherwise agree, the date directed by the committee. But in the case of an adjustment of rent, in the absence of agreement between the landlord and the tenant, the committee cannot direct a date earlier than the date specified in the notice.

The parties may by written notice to the committee terminate the reference either because they no longer want a determination or because the tenancy has come to an end.

A statutory periodic tenancy does not arise if, on the coming to an end of the fixed term tenancy, the tenant is entitled, by virtue of the grant of another tenancy, to possession of the same or substantially the same dwelling-house as was let to him under the fixed term tenancy.

As has been seen under "qualifying conditions" "Crown tenancies" and "local authority tenancies etc." cannot be assured tenancies. Provision is made in sections 5 and 6 with the result that such statutory periodic tenancies likewise cannot be assured tenancies.

If at any time on or before the date on which a fixed term tenancy or a periodic tenancy is entered into or at any time during the currency of a fixed term tenancy the person who is to be or is the tenant under that tenancy:

(a) enters into an obligation to do any act which apart from the Act would cause the tenancy to come to an end at a time when it is an assured tenancy; or

(b) executes, signs or gives any surrender, notice to quit or other document which apart from the Act would have the effect of bringing the tenancy to an end at a time when it is an assured tenancy, the obligation referred to is not enforceable or, as the case may be, the surrender, notice to quit or other such document has no effect.

These provisions are markedly different in wording from the provisions in section 38 of the 1954 Act (restrictions on agreements excluding provisions of Part II) but their effect will be substantially the same.

Any device which purports to have the effect of depriving a tenant of his security of tenure is likely to be held of no effect.

The decision in *Allnatt London Properties Limited* v. *Newton* (1980) 275 Estates Gazette 174 [1981] 2 AER 290 (the Vice Chancellor) affirmed by the Court of Appeal (1983) 265 Estates Gazette 601 [1984] 1 AER 423 may be applicable. Sir Robert Megarry held that a covenant in a lease stipulating that if a tenant desired to assign or underlet the demised premises he had to offer to surrender his lease to the landlord in consideration of a payment by the landlord of the net premium (if any) of the lease for the unexpired residue of the lease did not in itself offend against section 39(1) because it did not purport to preclude the tenant from making an application or request under Part II. But an agreement entered into for a surrender of the lease did offend and was void.

It is important to appreciate that a statutory periodic tenancy does not come into being on the termination of an assured contractual periodic tenancy. By a late amendment of section 5(1) a notice to quit served by a landlord is ineffective. But a tenant may serve such a notice and on its expiry he ceases to have an assured tenancy or indeed any tenancy. Thus section 7 does not apply. If the tenant does not quit on due date the landlord has an immediate right to possession which he may enforce in the courts.

During the continuance of an assured fixed term tenancy or a contractual periodic tenancy (whether created *ab initio* or coming into force on the ending of a fixed term tenancy by virtue of its express provisions) the provisions of section 6 (fixing of terms of statutory periodic tenancy) cannot be invoked. A landlord may seek to increase the rent during the continuance of a contractual periodic tenancy which contains no rent review provisions, but he cannot do so in respect of a fixed term tenancy lacking such provisions.

Rent under periodic assured tenancies

At the date of the initial letting and, subject to sections 13–16 of the 1988 Act, during the continuance of the tenancy the rent under the tenancy is the amount agreed between the parties but there are provisions in section 13 of the Act for seeking an increase in rent under the assured periodic tenancy. These provisions which enable a landlord under an assured tenancy to serve a notice on the assured tenant proposing a new rent apply to (i) a statutory periodic tenancy and (ii) any other assured periodic tenancy which does not have a provision under which the rent for a particular period will or may be greater than the rent for an earlier period, namely a provision for reviewing the rent.

Provisions under the 1988 Act for increasing the rent

In the case of a statutory periodic tenancy or any other periodic tenancy which does not have a provision for reviewing the rent the landlord may serve on the tenant a notice proposing a new rent to take effect at the beginning of a new period of the tenancy specified in the notice. However, the new period must not begin earlier than:

    (a) the minimum period after the date of the service of the notice which is
        (i)   six months in the case of a yearly tenancy;
        (ii) one month in the case of a periodic tenancy of less than one month;
        (iii) a period equal to the period of the tenancy in any other case; and
    (b) the first anniversary of the date on which the first period of the tenancy began (except in the case of a statutory periodic tenancy) and
    (c) if the rent under the tenancy had previously been increased, by a notice under section 13(2) or a determination under

section 14, the first anniversary of the date on which the increased rent took effect.

There is a prescribed form for the landlord's notice under section 13(2) of the 1988 Act which is to be found at Appendix A.

Where a notice has been served under section 13(2) the new rent takes effect as specified in that notice unless before the beginning of the new period either (i) the tenant refers the notice to a rent assessment committee or (ii) the landlord and tenant agree on a variation of the rent which is different from that proposed in the notice or agree that the rent should not be varied.

Determination of rent by a rent assessment committee

If a tenant under an assured tenancy has received a notice proposing a new rent which satisfies section 13(2) of the 1988 Act an assured tenant may refer the notice to a rent assessment committee. The rent assessment committee is to determine the rent at which it considers that the dwelling-house concerned might reasonably be expected to let in the open market by a willing landlord under an assured tenancy; section 14(1). There is no definition of the term "willing landlord" in the 1988 Act but it has been considered in the context of rent review. In *F. R. Evans (Leeds) Ltd.* v. *English Electric Co. Ltd.* (1977) 245 EG 657 Donaldson J. (as he then was) held that the term "willing lessor" was an abstraction, a hypothetical person with a right to grant a lease of the premises who wants to let the premises at an appropriate rent but who is not afflicted by personal difficulties such as a cash flow crisis. In *Dennis & Robinson Ltd.* v. *Kiossos Establishment* [1987] 1 EGLR 131 (a case involving rent review) the Court of Appeal was of the opinion that a requirement to determine an open market rent necessarily imports the assumption of a willing lessee and a willing lessor. However, it is a matter for the valuer (using his experience and judgment) to determine the strength of the market and there is no assumption as to the state of the market. The assured tenancy to be considered is one which satisfies the following qualifications, namely (section 14(2)).

(a) which is a periodic tenancy having the same periods as those of the tenancy to which the notice relates;

(b) which begins at the beginning of the new period specified in the notice;

(c) the terms of which (other than those relating to the amount of the rent) are the same as those of the tenancy to which the notice relates; and

(d) in respect of which the same notices, if any, have been given under any of Grounds 1 to 5 of Part I, Schedule 2 to this Act, as have been given (or have effect as if given) in relation to the tenancy to which the notice relates.

In the context of the provisions of section 14 the word "rent" does not include any service charge within the meaning of section 18 of the Landlord and Tenant Act 1985 but includes any sums payable by the tenant to the landlord on account of the use of furniture or for any of the matters referred to in section 18(1)(a) of that 1985 Act whether or not payable separately. If any rates in respect of the dwelling-house concerned are borne by the landlord or a superior landlord the rent assessment committee is to make its determination as if the rates were not so borne.

In making a determination for the purposes of section 14, the rent assessment committee must disregard the following:

"(a) any effect on the rent attributable to the granting of a tenancy to a sitting tenant;

(b) any increase in the value of the dwelling-house attributable to a relevant improvement carried out by a person who at the time it was carried out was the tenant, if the improvement—

  (i) was carried out otherwise than in pursuance of an obligation to his immediate landlord, or

  (ii) was carried out pursuant to an obligation to his immediate landlord being an obligation which did not relate to the specific improvement concerned but arose by reference to consent given to the carrying out of that improvement; and

(c) any reduction in the value of the dwelling-house attributable to a failure by the tenant to comply with any terms of the tenancy."

A "relevant improvement" for the purposes of section 14(2)(b) of the 1988 Act is one which either was carried out during the tenancy to which the notice being referred to the rent assessment committee relates or which satisfies the following conditions, namely;

(a) that it was carried out not more than twenty-one years before the date of service of the notice; and

(b) that, at all times during the period beginning when the improvement was carried out and ending on the date of service of the notice, the dwelling-house has been let under an assured tenancy; and

(c) that, on the coming to an end of an assured tenancy at

any time during that period, the tenant (or, in the case
of joint tenants, at least one of them) did not quit.

The provisions contained in section 14(2),(3) of the 1988 Act are
somewhat complex and contain elements of the disregards applicable under section 34 of the 1954 Act. There is no definition of
"improvement" in the 1988 Act but in interpreting the phrase under
the Landlord and Tenant Act 1927 it has been held that whether
works to the demised premises constitute an improvement should
be considered from the tenant's viewpoint; *Lambert* v. *F. W. Wool-
worth & Co. Ltd. (No. 2)* (1938) Ch. 883. Further, demolition
and reconstruction can amount to an improvement; *National Electric Theatres Ltd.* v. *Hudgell* ([1939] Ch. 249) 133 EG 273.

If a notice to increase the rent under section 13(2) has been referred to the rent assessment committee the rent determined by the
committee is the rent under the tenancy with effect from the beginning of the new period specified in the notice or such later date
as the committee may direct (not being later than the date the rent
is determined) if it appears to the committee that the date of the
new period specified in the notice would cause undue hardship to
the tenant. It is open to the landlord and tenant to agree when
the rent under the tenancy will take effect; section 14(7) of the
1988 Act. In addition, the landlord and tenant may give notice
to the rent assessment committee that they no longer require the
determination of the rent and there are similar provisions where
the tenancy has come to an end; section 14(8) of the 1988 Act.
It is to be noted that there are administrative and procedural changes
to the work of rent assessment committeess contained in sections
41 and 42 of the 1988 Act.

Varying the terms of assured periodic tenancies

It is possible for the landlord and tenant under an assured tenancy
to vary by agreement any term of the tenancy including a term
relating to rent; section 13(5) of the 1988 Act. It thus appears that
the parties can agree on the inclusion of a clause allowing the revision
of rent but the most appropriate form of rent review provision for
inclusion in an assured tenancy is an important aspect. It may be
that the provision for the revision of rent in such a tenancy would
be more appropriately linked with an index such as the Retail Price
Index or other similar indexation scale. In other cases, a more conventional form of rent review clause may be more appropriate where
the assured periodic tenancy is of a longer term e.g. by a valuer.

Rent under fixed term assured tenancies

The provisions of section 13(2) of the 1988 Act do not apply in the case of fixed term assured tenancies so that rent review provisions should be included in such tenancies. Where the fixed term is of a fairly short length it may be that the provision as to rent review would be most appropriately satisfied by being linked to an index. In the case of a longer fixed term assured tenancy a more conventional form of rent review clause may be more appropriate. In such a case regard should be had to the following factors, namely:

(1) Stipulations as to time in the service of notices.
(2) Interval of rent review.
(3) Formula and machinery for determining the new rent.
(4) Provisions in event of disagreement.

Service of notices

It is frequently the case that the rent review procedure is activated by the service of a "trigger" notice which commences the rent review process. In most cases, the notice will be served by the landlord on the tenant and the main problem that has arisen in this area is whether a failure to keep strictly to the timetable set in the rent review clause will result in the landlord losing his rights to a reviewed rent. In *United Scientific Holdings Ltd.* v. *Burnley Corporation* [1977] 2 All ER 62, the House of Lords laid down the general rule that time was not of the essence in the service of notices in a rent review process, but stated that there could be exceptions to this general rule. It is possible to make time of the essence by stating expressly in the lease that it should be so, but time can also be made of the essence where there is an interrelationship between the rent review clause and some other clause in the lease. Such was the case in *Al Saloom* v. *Shirley James Travel* (1981) 259 EG 420 where an underlease contained both a break clause and a rent review clause and the last date on which the landlord could serve the rent review notice was the same as that on which the tenant could give notice exercising his option to determine the underlease. In these circumstances, it was held that the presence of the break clause had the effect of making time of the essence. Where the lease provides for a period between service of the rent review notice and the exercise of the break clause, so as to allow the tenant to determine whether he wishes to continue in occupation, the service of the rent review notice will be of the essence. In *United Scientific (supra)* it was suggested that extreme delay in the service of a trigger notice may have a prejudicial effect on the landlord's cause. The question of what constitutes unreasonable delay has arisen on several occasions. In *H. West* v. *Brech* (1982) 261 EG 156 a delay of 18 months was not sufficient to affect the landlord's rights (see also *Accuba* v. *Allied Shoe Repairs* [1975] 1 WLR 1559 where also 18 months delay was insufficient and contrast with *Telegraph Properties (Securities)* v. *Courtaulds* (1980) 257 EG 1153 where a six year delay was fatal to the landlord's action). More recently in *Amherst* v. *James Walker (Goldsmith and Silversmith) Ltd.* (1983) 267 EG 163 Oliver, L.J. commented:

> "But I know of no ground for saying that mere delay, however lengthy, destroys the contractual right. It may put the other party in a position, where, by taking the proper steps, he may become entitled to treat himself as discharged from his obligation: but that does not occur automatically and from the mere passage of time . . ."

In *United Scientific (supra)* the House of Lords recognised that a contra-indication may make time of the essence for the service of a rent review trigger-notice. What amounts to a contra-indication is the subject of dispute. In *Henry Smith's Charity Trustees* v. *A.W.A.D.A. Trading and Promotion Services Ltd.* (1983) 269 EG 729 the clause contained an elaborate time schedule and provided that the rent stated by the landlord be deemed to be the rent if the tenant's counter-notice was not served in time. The Court of Appeal held that where the parties had not only set out a timetable but had provided what was to happen in the absence of strict compliance with that timetable the general rule was rebutted. The Court of Appeal reached a different conclusion in the interpretation of a "deeming" provision in *Mecca Leisure Ltd.* v. *Renown Investments (Holdings) Ltd.* (1984) 271 EG 989. In *Greenhaven Securities Ltd.* v. *Compton* (1985) 275 EG 628 the rent review clause provided that if the parties had not, within a 15 month time limit, agreed on an arbitrator or made an application for the appointment of an arbitrator the new rent should be a sum equal to the old rent. Goulding J. distinguished the decision in *Mecca* and held that the default provision constituted a contra-indication. The opposite view was taken in *Taylor Woodrow Property Co. Ltd.* v. *Lonrho Textiles Ltd.* (1985) 275 EG 632 where the court noted that in *Henry Smith's* the deeming provisions were two-way whilst in *Mecca* they were one-way. In *Taylor Woodrow* the deeming provision was one-way so that time was not of the essence in the service of the counter-notice.

Interval of rent review

It is clearly important for the interval of rent review to be expressly stated so that, for example, on a 21 year lease the rent review clause may become operative in the 7th and 14th years. Where it is not so, the rent review clause runs the risk of being inoperable. In *Brown* v. *Gould* [1972] Ch. 53 the option for a new lease was for a term of 21 years "at a rent to be fixed, having regard to the market value of the premises at the time of exercising the option". The court held that if no machinery was stated for working out the formula, the court will determine the matter itself. A liberal approach to the construction of an option to purchase was adopted in *Sudbrook Trading Estate Ltd.* v. *Eggleton* (1983) 265 EG 215.

Formula and machinery

The formula and machinery has, of necessity, a direct relationship with the interval of rent review. Valuers are faced with enough problems on rent review without the clause adding to those problems by failing to define the rental on review. Such was the case in *Beer* v. *Bowden* [1981] 1 All ER 1070 where the clause provided only that the rent should be the fair market rent for the premises. In the particular circumstances of the case the Court of Appeal stated that the rent should be the fair market rent for the premises. See also *Thomas Bates and Sons Ltd.* v. *Wyndhams Lingerie Ltd.* [1981] 1 All ER 1077 where a term was implied that the rent was to be that which is "reasonable as between the parties". By way of contrast, in *King* v. *King* (1980) 255 EG 1205 the court refused to look at the defective rent review clause from a reasonableness viewpoint.

Some novel provisions on rent are being considered by draftsmen seeking to increase the landlord's benefit as in *Bovis Group Pension Fund Ltd.* v. *G.C. Flooring and Furnishing Ltd.* (1983) 266 EG 1005 where the clause provided for the new rent to be assessed by reference to the rent that could be obtained if the premises were let for office purposes and the court stated that it was to be assumed that the building had planning permission for office use notwithstanding that no such permission had, in fact, been granted. Similarly, in *Pugh* v. *Smiths Industries* (1982) 264 EG 823 it was held that the rent review should be on a literal construction of the lease where the formula provided that the presence of the review clause should be disregarded in calculating the new rent (see also *Lister Locks Ltd.* v. *T.E.I. Pension Trust Ltd.* (1982) 264 EG 827). The converse situation applied in *GREA Real Property Investments Ltd.* v. *Williams* (1979) 250 EG 651 where it was decided that the effect of improvements on a rent review of premises in shell-form only had to be disregarded. If no such improvements disregard clause is present, the tenant will have to pay increased rent on his own improvements (contrast with the situation on a lease renewed under section 34 of the 1954 Act). If a strict user clause is present in the lease, this may also have a dampening effect on the new rental level as in *Plinth Property Investments* v. *Mott, Hay and Anderson* (1978) 249 EG 1167. See also *Law Land Co. Ltd.* v. *Consumers' Association Ltd.* (1980) 255 EG 617. The factors contained in the hypothetical lease for the purpose of the determination of the revised rent may pose problems for the valuer. In *National Westminster Bank plc* v. *Arthur Young McClelland Moores & Co.* (1984) 273 EG 402 the court held that in that particular lease the fair market rent had to be ascertained on the assumption that there was no rent revision clause contained in the hypothetical terms which the arbitrator had to apply. A similar conclusion was reached (at first instance) in *Equity & Law Life Assurance Society plc* v. *Bodfield Ltd.* (1985) 276 EG 1157. Different conclusions from these two cases were reached in *Datastream International Ltd.* v. *Oakeep Ltd.* (1985) 277 EG 66 and *M.F.I. Properties Ltd.* v. *B.I.C.C. Group Pension Trust Ltd.* (1986) 277 EG 862. In *British Gas Corporation* v. *Universities Superannuation Scheme Ltd.* (1986) 277 EG 980 Browne-Wilkinson V.C. said that the correct approach in these circumstances was as follows:

"(a) words in a rent exclusion provision which require *all* provisions as to rent to be disregarded produced a result so manifestly contrary to commercial common sense that they cannot be given literal effect;

(b) other clear words which require the rent review provision (as opposed to all provisions as to rent) to be disregarded must be given effect to, however wayward the result; and

(c) subject to (b), in the absence of special circumstances it is proper to give effect to the underlying commercial purpose of a rent review clause and to construe the words so as to give effect to that purpose by requiring future rent reviews to be taken into account in fixing the open market rental under the hypothetical letting."

These were stressed as being only "guidelines" by the Court of Appeal in the *Equity and Law Life* case [1987] 1 EGLR 124.

Disagreement

A well drafted rent review clause should always provide for a procedure in event of disagreement between the landlord and tenant on the new rental level. It should be made clear whether reference to an arbitrator or independent expert is desired.

Chapter 6
Succession

(a) In respect of assured tenancies

Somewhat surprisingly when the Bill was published no provision was made to protect a person whose tenant spouse died. This lacuna was made good on the Report stage.

Protection is now achieved by section 17 whereby a tenancy vests in a spouse and does not devolve upon him or her under the tenant's will or on an intestacy.

The section does not apply to fixed term tenancies where the ordinary law relating to devolution by will or on an intestacy remains unaffected.

Although a contractual periodic tenancy can devolve by will or on an intestacy it was obviously considered desirable that both contractual and statutory periodic tenancies should be dealt with in the same manner.

Of course the original tenancy must always be an assured tenancy for the purposes of section 17.

The surviving spouse must at the time of the tenant's death have been occupying the dwelling-house as his or her only or principal home.

A spouse within the section is given a wide meaning: namely a person who was living with the tenant as his or her wife or husband. The legislature contemplates that two men or two women may be occupying the dwelling-house as their only or principal home and vie for the description of the surviving spouse. In the absence of agreement the court has the task of Solomon to determine which shall be treated as the tenant's spouse for the purposes of this section.

The succession protected by this section is given only once to a tenancy.

Thus if in his lifetime the dead tenant inherited a fixed term assured tenancy under a will or on an intestacy or had vested in him a periodic tenancy by virtue of this section no further protection is afforded.

Provisions are also made for the position of a joint tenancy.

The loss of protection is extended to what is called a "new tenancy". Where the circumstances are those set out in the penultimate paragraph and the successor tenant is granted alone or jointly with others a tenancy consisting of a dwelling-house or a tenancy of a dwelling-house which is substantially the same as that dwelling-house and there is no break in occupation between the end of the succeeded tenancy and the new tenancy, there is no protection.

(b)   In respect of certain tenancies previously protected by the 1977 Act or the 1976 Act

Section 39 of and Schedule 4 to the 1988 Act contain important provisions which will result in certain persons who would have become statutory tenants under the Rent Act on the death of an original or first successor tenant becoming entitled instead to an assured tenancy.

The provisions are important because the tenant will not be entitled to the rent control protection he would have enjoyed as a statutory tenant and the grounds on which the landlord will become entitled to possession are also significantly different.

Further persons who might have become statutory tenants on succession will now lose their protection altogether.

Under section 2(1) of Part I of Schedule 1 to the 1977 Act as amended there may be a maximum of two transmissions on death; first on the death of an original tenant, the second on the death of the first successor.

In each case, at least since the relevant provisions of the 1980 Act came into force, the surviving spouse of the deceased tenant succeeds if he or she was residing with her or him at death. If, however, there is no surviving spouse a member of the tenant's family may succeed providing he or she was residing with the tenant at the time of her or his death and for six months preceding the tenant's death.

Now, however, on the death of an original tenant or a first successor which occurs after the 14th January 1989 significantly different rules will apply to those applying before that date.

Where the death is that of the original tenant Part I of Schedule 1 to the 1977 Act has effect subject to the amendments in Part I to Schedule 4 to the 1988 Act. Where, however, it is the first successor who dies Part I of Schedule 1 to the 1977 Act has effect subject to the amendments in paragraphs 5 to 9 of Part I of Schedule 4 to the 1988 Act.

So that the effect of the amendments may be appreciated Part I of Schedule 1 to the 1977 Act with the amendments of Part I of Schedule 4 to the 1988 Act is printed as Appendix B.

Provision is made defining a spouse of a deceased original

tenant. Where there is no such spouse a member of the family may succeed but he or she must have been residing in the dwelling-house at the time of the death and for the period of two years before the death. Transitional periods are made where the original tenant dies within eighteen months of the 15th January 1989.

When the first successor was a protected tenant at the time of his death then a surviving spouse and a member of the family are both treated in like manner to that of a member of the family on the death of the original tenant.

In the case of an original occupier within the meaning of section 4 of the 1976 Act (statutory tenants and tenancies) who dies after the 14th January 1989 that section has effect subject to the amendments in Part II of Schedule 4 to the 1988 Act.

That section contains provisions not dissimilar to those contained in Part I of Schedule 1 to the 1977 Act insofar as they relate to successors on the death of an original tenant. The amendment to section 4 on the death of an occupier after the 14th January 1989 will result in a person who is entitled to possession becoming entitled to an assured tenancy. Again for an understanding of the position section 4 is printed as amended in Appendix C.

The periodic assured tenancy to which such a successor becomes entitled is one:

(a) taking effect in possession immediately after the death of the protected or statutory tenant or protected occupier called "the predecessor" on whose death the successor became so entitled;

(b) deemed to have been granted to the successor by the person who, immediately before the death of the predecessor, was the landlord of the predecessor under his tenancy;

(c) under which the premises which are let are the same dwelling-house as, immediately before his death, the predecessor occupied under his tenancy;

(d) under which the periods of the tenancy are the same as those for which rent was last payable by the predecessor under his tenancy;

(e) under which subject to section 13 (increase of rent under assured periodic tenancies), section 14 (determination of rent by rent assessment committee) and section 15 (the limited prohibition on assignment etc. without consent) the other terms are the same as those on which, under his tenancy, the predecessor occupied the dwelling-house immediately before his death; and

(f) which for the purposes of section 13(2) (landlord's notice

for the purpose of securing an increase in rent) is treated
as a statutory periodic tenancy.

In paragraphs (b) to (c) "under his tenancy" in relation to the
predecessor means under his protected tenancy or protected occupancy or in his capacity as a statutory tenant.

If immediately before the death of the predecessor, the landlord
might have recovered possession of the dwelling-house under Case
19 of Schedule 15 to the 1977 Act (dwelling-house let under a
protected shorthold tenancy or is treated under section 55 of the
1980 Act as having been so let) the assured periodic tenancy to
which the successor becomes entitled is to be an assured shorthold
tenancy (whether or not it fulfils the conditions in section 20(1)—
definition of assured shorthold tenancies).

If immediately before his death, the predecessor was a protected
occupier or statutory tenant within the meaning of the 1976 Act
the assured periodic tenancy to which the successor becomes entitled
shall be an assured agricultural occupancy (whether or not it fulfils
the conditions of section 24(1)—definition of assured agricultural
occupancies).

Provision is also made where a protected or statutory tenant or
protected tenant (the predecessor) was a tenant under a fixed term
tenancy. Section 6 (fixing of terms of statutory periodic tenancy)
is to apply in relation to the assured periodic tenancy to which
the successor becomes entitled on the predecessor's death but subject
to certain modifications.

For any reference to a statutory periodic tenancy there is to be
substituted a reference to the assured periodic tenancy to which
the successor becomes so entitled. The definition of "the former
tenancy" in section 6(1)(a) is omitted. The definition of "implied
terms" means the terms of the tenancy which have effect by virtue
of section 39(6)(e) not section 5(3)(e).

Finally for any reference to the coming to an end of the former
tenancy there is to be substituted a reference to the date of the
predecessor's death.

Mandatory grounds of possession

Section 7 of and Schedule 2 to the 1988 Act provide a code for obtaining possession which differs significantly from that contained in the 1977 Act governing controlled or regulated tenancies, from that contained in Part II of the 1954 Act governing business tenancies and from that in the 1980 Act governing the mark 1 assured tenancies. But in the course of its passage through the House of Commons the Bill was significantly altered in favour of the tenant.

Grounds for possession are divided into those in which the court has no discretion and those in which it has. The former—eight in number—are set out in Part I Schedule 2 as Grounds 1–8; the latter—eight in number— are set out in Part II as Grounds 9–16. Before amendment in the House of Commons the respective figures were 10 and 6.

Once the court is satisfied that any Part 1 Ground is established the court must make an order for possession. In the case, however, of Part II Grounds, the position remains as it is under Part I of Schedule 15 to the 1977 Act. Even though the court is satisfied that a Ground is established it may only make an order if it considers it reasonable to do so.

The reason why the 1988 Act differs in its grounds for possession for assured tenancies from those governing assured tenancies in the 1980 Act is no doubt because the various grounds of possession contained in section 30 of Part II of the 1954 Act have not proved to be entirely suitable. They were devised to deal with business tenancies and are not always appropriate for residential tenancies.

By section 12, introduced during the Committee stage in the House of Commons, an order for possession under Schedule 2 obtained by misrepresentation or concealment of material facts, may result in the landlord being ordered to pay the former tenant such sum as appears sufficient as compensation for damage or loss sustained by him as a result of that order. These provisions mirror those contained in section 55 of the 1954 Act.

The order for possession cannot take effect at a time when the dwelling-house is let as an assured fixed term tenancy save in respect

of Ground 2 or 8 in Part I of Schedule 2 or of any of the grounds
in Part II other than Ground 16 and the terms of the tenancy make
provision for it to be brought to an end on the ground in question
(whether that provision takes the form of a provision for re-entry,
for forfeiture, determination by notice or otherwise).

But where a fixed term tenancy has ended, any statutory periodic
tenancy which has arisen on the ending of the fixed term tenancy
shall end (without any notice and regardless of the period) on the
day on which the order for possession takes place.

Ground 1

"Not later than the beginning of the tenancy the landlord gave
notice in writing to the tenant that possession might be recovered
on this ground or the court is of the opinion that it is just and
equitable to dispense with the requirement of notice and (in either case):

    (a) at some time before the beginning of the tenancy, the land-
lord who is seeking possession or, in the case of joint landlords seeking possession, at least one of them occupied the
dwelling-house as his only or principal home; or

    (b) the landlord who is seeking possession or, in the case of
joint landlords seeking possession, at least one of them
requires the dwelling-house as his or his spouse's only or
principal home and neither the landlord (or, in the case
of joint landlords, any one of them) nor any other person
who, as landlord, derived title under the landlord who gave
the notice mentioned above acquired the reversion on the
tenancy for money or money's worth."

These provisions differ markedly from those contained in section
30(1)(g) and (h) of Part II of the 1954 Act.

Case 9 in Schedule 15 to the 1977 Act gives a court discretion
to make an order for possession where the premises are reasonably
required by the landlord or certain members of his family so
long as the landlord had not become so by purchase before certain
dates depending on the type of tenancy. Further by Part III of
Schedule 15 the court has to consider the question of greater
hardship.

Case 11 in Part V of the same Schedule, as amended by the Rent
(Amendment) Act 1985, made provision for the recovery of possession of an owner-occupied house subject to a regulated tenancy.

The landlord proceeding under Case 9 had two hurdles to sur-
mount. He had to establish that the dwelling-house was reasonably
required. Further the court had to be satisfied that it was reasonable

to make the order. Neither such hurdle stood in the path of the landlord proceeding under Case 11.

In certain respects the provisions of the present Ground 1 are simpler than those contained in Case 11 but in other respects, particularly as regards the conditions in Part V, the Ground 1 provisions are significantly narrower.

To succeed under this ground the landlord, or in the case of joint landlords at least one of them, must establish that the dwelling-house is required as his or his spouse's only or principal home. The reversion to the assured tenancy sought to be ended must not have been acquired for money or money's worth.

The notice required to be given should identify the ground under which possession might be recovered and the occasion therefor and stress that a court order if necessary might be sought.

The words "at some time" in (a) indicates that the landlord's previous occupation need not be immediately prior to the granting of the assured tenancy.

Ground 2

"The dwelling-house is subject to a mortgage granted before the beginning of the tenancy and:

    (a) the mortgagee is entitled to exercise a power of sale conferred on him by the mortgage or by section 101 of the Law of Property Act 1925; and

    (b) the mortgagee requires possession of the dwelling-house for the purpose of disposing of it with vacant possession in exercise of that power; and

    (c) either notice was given as mentioned in Ground 1 above or the court is satisfied that it is just and equitable to dispense with the requirement of notice

and for the purposes of this ground 'mortgage' includes a charge and 'mortgagee' shall be construed accordingly."

In actions for possession under the 1977 Act brought pursuant to Cases 11, 12 and 20(e)(ii) the court is bound to make an order if condition 2(e) of Part V of Schedule 15 of the 1977 Act is established. Ground 2 contains substantially similar provisions.

It is to be noted that the notice required is that mentioned in Ground 1. There was a very late amendment to section 7(1) of this Act. This provided that as regards assured tenancies nothing in the Act relates to proceedings for possession of a dwelling-house which are brought by a mortgagee, within the meaning of the law of Property Act 1925, who had lent money on the security of the assured tenancy.

Ground 3

"The tenancy is a fixed term tenancy for a term not exceeding eight months and:

(a) not later than the beginning of the tenancy the landlord gave notice in writing to the tenant that possession might be recovered on this ground; and

(b) at some time within the period of twelve months ending with the beginning of the tenancy, the dwelling-house was occupied under a right to occupy it for a holiday."

The provisions are not dissimilar to those contained in Case 13 in Schedule 15 to the 1977 Act. Further the provisions of paragraph 9 of Part I of Schedule 1 to the 1988 Act have essentially the same effect as the provisions of section 9 of the 1977 Act. The effect is that a tenancy of a holiday letting cannot be an assured tenancy and the landlord may recover possession of a short tenancy of a holiday home within Ground 3 without establishing reasonableness.

Ground 4

"The tenancy is a fixed term tenancy for a term not exceeding twelve months and:

(a) not later than the beginning of the tenancy the landlord gave notice in writing to the tenant that possession might be recovered on this ground; and

(b) at some time within the period of twelve months ending with the beginning of the tenancy, the dwelling-house was let on a tenancy falling within paragraph 8 of Schedule 1 to this Act."

Paragraph 8(1) of Part I of Schedule 1 to the 1988 Act mirrors section 8(1) of the 1977 Act in the same way as Ground 4 mirrors Case 14 of Schedule 15 to the 1977 Act.

A paragraph 8(1) tenancy cannot be assured tenancy while Ground 4 entitles the landlord to an order for possession without having to show reasonableness.

Ground 5

"The dwelling-house is held for the purpose of being available for occupation by a minister of religion as a residence from which to perform the duties of his office and:

(a) not later than the beginning of the tenancy the landlord gave notice in writing to the tenant that possession might be recovered on this ground; and

(b) the court is satisfied that the dwelling-house is required for occupation by a minister of religion as such a residence."

These provisions follow those in Case 15 of Schedule 15 to the 1977 Act. In neither case does reasonableness have to be established.

Ground 6

"The landlord who is seeking possession or, if that landlord is a registered housing association or charitable housing trust, a superior landlord intends to demolish or reconstruct the whole or a substantial part of the dwelling-house or to carry out substantial works on the dwelling-house or any part thereof or any building of which it forms part and the following conditions are fulfilled:

(a) the intended work cannot reasonably be carried out without the tenant giving up possession of the dwelling-house because:

(i) the tenant is not willing to agree to such a variation of the terms of the tenancy as would give such access and other facilities as would permit the intended work to be carried out, or

(ii) the nature of the intended work is such that no such variation is practicable, or

(iii) the tenant is not willing to accept an assured tenancy of such part only of the dwelling-house (in this sub-paragraph referred to as 'the reduced part') as would leave in the possession of his landlord so much of the dwelling-house as would be reasonable to enable the intended work to be carried out and, where appropriate, as would give such access and other facilities over the reduced part as would permit the intended work to be carried out, or

(iv) the nature of the intended work is such that such a tenancy is not practicable; and

(b) either the landlord seeking possession acquired his interest in the dwelling-house before the grant of the tenancy or that interest was in existence at the time of that grant and neither the landlord (or, in the case of joint landlords, any of them) nor any person who, alone or jointly with others, has acquired that interest since that time acquired it for money or money's worth; and

(c) the assured tenancy on which the dwelling-house is let did not come into being by virtue of any provision of Schedule 1 to the Rent Act 1977, as amended by Part I of Schedule 4 to this Act or, as the case may be, section 4 of the Rent (Agriculture) Act 1976, as amended by Part II of that Schedule.

For the purposes of this ground if, immediately before the grant of the tenancy, the tenant to whom it was granted or, if it was granted to joint tenants, any of them was the tenant or one of the joint tenants under an earlier assured tenancy of the dwelling-house concerned, any reference to paragraph (b) above to the grant of the tenancy is a reference to the grant of that earlier assured tenancy.

For the purposes of this ground 'registered housing association' has the same meaning as in the Housing Associations Act 1985 and 'charitable housing trust' means a housing trust, within the meaning of that Act, which is a charity, within the meaning of the Charities Act 1960."

There are no similar provisions in the 1977 Act. Ground 6 has a number of similarities to the provisions in sections 30(1)(f) and 31A of the 1954 Act which apply to business tenancies.

Whilst it is unlikely that Ground 6 will generate as much litigation as section 30(i)(f)—not least because litigation under that section has resolved many of the uncertainties arising from its wording —nevertheless it is likely to be a litigious ground because whether or not a landlord has formed the necessary intent in the nature of things may give rise to a dispute.

In *Cunliffe* v.*Goodman* [1950] 2 KB 237 which was a decision on section 18(1) of the Landlord and Tenant Act 1927 Asquith L. J. at p. 253 said:

> "An 'intention' to my mind connotes a state of affairs which the party 'intending'—I will call him X— does more than merely contemplate: it connotes a state of affairs which, on the contrary, he decides so far as in him lies, to bring about, and which in point of possibility, he has a reasonable prospect of being able to bring about by his own act of volition."

At p. 254 he said:

> "Not merely is the 'intention' unsatisfied if the person professing it has too many hurdles to overcome, or too little control of events; it is equally inappropriate if at the material date that person is in effect not deciding to proceed but feeling his way and reserving his decision until he shall be in possession

of financial data sufficient to enable him to determine whether
the payment will be commercially worthwhile."

"In the case of neither scheme did she form a settled intention
to proceed. Neither project moved out of the zone of contemplation—out of the sphere of the tentative, the provisional and
the exploratory—into the valley of decision."

This definition was approved for the purposes of paragraph (f)
of section 30 by Viscount Simmonds in *Betty's Cafes, Limited* v.
Phillip Furnishing Stores Limited 171 Estates Gazette 319 [1959]
AC 20.

For other numerous decisions under Part II of the 1954 Act as
to whether a sufficient intention has been established see Business
Tenancies by James Fox-Andrews, published by Estates Gazette.

It was held in *Betty's Cafes* case that the intention has to be
shown to exist at the time of the hearing. The same position would
appear to obtain here. The time at which the landlord is required
to put his intention into effect is not stipulated unlike the position
under (f) where it was at the date of the termination of the current
tenancy. Nevertheless it would seem likely that the intention established at the hearing must be one that takes effect at or shortly
after the obtaining of possession.

Under the 1988 Act the landlord is in a position to ensure that
the action for possession comes on for hearing at a time of his
choosing. This was not necessarily the case under Part II of the
1954 Act particularly where the tenancy was brought to an end
by a tenant's request under section 26. It is no doubt partly because
the landlord can select the time at which his application for possession will come on that the 1988 Act does not contain provisions
similar to those contained in section 31(2) of the 1954 Act.

The words "to demolish or reconstruct the whole or a substantial
part of the dwelling-house or to carry out substantial works on
the dwelling-house or any part thereof or any building of which it
forms part" are to be contrasted with the words in paragraph (f):

> "to demolish or reconstruct the premises comprised in the hold-
> ing or a substantial part of those premises or to carry
> out substantial work of construction on the holding or part
> thereof."

On the paragraph (f) wording the Court of Appeal held in *Cadle
(Percy E.) and Co. Limited* v. *Jacmarch Properties Limited* 168
Estates Gazette 669 [1957] 1 QB 323 that the word "reconstruct"
meant a physical rebuilding following a measure of demolition of
the premises comprised in the holding. A mere change of identity
was not enough.

In *Cook* v. *Mott* (1961) 178 Estates Gazette 637, the Court of Appeal considered that reconstruction postulated a demolition in whole or in part of an existing structure but that "construction" embraced new or additional work.

The nature of the substantial works in Ground 6 is not restricted to works of construction as they are in paragraph (f).

The words in Ground 6 "any building of which it forms part" do not find an echo in the paragraph (f) provisions.

Where a landlord wishes to carry out substantial works on a block of flats he owns and possession is necessary of the whole building although in fact no work will be done on the premises comprised in a particular assured tenancy this ground will be available to him. This however is subject to the effect of certain conditions to which Ground 6 is subject which are considered below.

The terms of condition (b) set out above will be noted. A landlord who derives his title on intestacy or under a will or by virtue of a gift will be unaffected.

The provisions of condition (a) are intended to overcome the difficulties that arose in respect of paragraph (f) and which led in 1969 to the inclusion of a new section 31A in the 1954 Act.

No problems arise where the terms of the assured tenancy include terms which give the landlord the required access and other facilities to enable him to reconstruct or carry out substantial works. See for example *Little Park Services Station, Limited* v. *Regent Oil Company* 201 Estates Gazette 585 [1967] 2 QB 655 CA.

It follows that in such a case a landlord will not be able to establish Ground 6 in any event; see *Heath* v. *Drown* 224 Estates Gazette 231 [1973] AC 498.

Where the tenancy agreement if varied to include such terms would enable the landlord to enter and execute the works but the tenant is not willing to accept such variation then Ground 6 will be available to the landlord.

Where a variation of the tenancy terms still would not enable the landlord to execute the works then the landlord may proceed under this ground.

As to condition (a)(iii) it does not appear that the requisite circumstances are likely to arise with much frequency. A tenancy comprising less in the way of accommodation than the original tenancy ("the reduced part") would probably only be acceptable to a tenant whose family had grown smaller.

In any case where condition (a) applies the landlord must establish that he could not reasonably have carried out the intended works without obtaining possession.

The reasonable requirements substantially match those in section 31A of the 1954 Act.

By section 11 where a court makes an order for possession on this ground the landlord has to pay a sum equal to the reasonable expense likely to be incurred by the tenant in removing from the dwelling-house.

If there is a dispute as to the amount of such sum it is to be determined by agreement between the landlord and the tenant or, in default of agreement, by the court.

Ground 7

"The tenancy was a periodic tenancy (including a statutory periodic tenancy) which has devolved under the will or intestacy of the former tenant and the proceedings for the recovery of possession are begun not later than twelve months after the death of the former tenant or, if a court so directs, after the date on which, in the opinion of the court, the landlord or, in the case of joint landlords, any one of them became aware of the former tenant's death.

For the purpose of this ground, the acceptance by the landlord of rent from a new tenant after the death of a former tenant shall not be regarded as creating a new periodic tenancy, unless the landlord agrees in writing to a change (as compared with the tenancy before the death) in the amount of the rent, the period of the tenancy, the premises which are let or any other term of the tenancy."

Under the 1980 Act the great majority of the assured tenancies were for fixed terms: indeed a large proportion were for terms of 21 years or more. On a monitoring exercise carried out by the Department of the Environment in respect of the position at 1st April 1987 out of 3,764 assured tenancies of which the Department had information only 137 were periodic tenancies. No yearly tenancies were apparently identified.

It is difficult to judge how many periodic tenancies will be granted under the 1988 Act, particularly those brought into being under Business Expansion Schemes. But on the coming to an end of a fixed term assured tenancy other than by virtue of an order of the court or a surrender or other action on the part of the tenant the fixed term tenancy becomes a periodic tenancy pursuant to section 5 and is defined as a statutory periodic tenancy and is a tenancy to which this ground for possession may apply.

There are no similar provisions in the 1977 Act or the 1954 Act.

For the purposes of this Ground 7, the acceptance by the landlord of rent from a tenant after the death of the former tenant is not to be regarded as creating a new periodic tenancy, unless the land-lord agrees in writing to a change (as compared with the terms of the tenancy before the death) in the amount of rent, the period of the tenancy, the premises which are let or any other terms of the tenancy.

By Ground 7 a tenant who has inherited a periodic tenancy will lose his tenancy so long as the landlord commences proceedings within the times laid down. Provision is made in the case of joint landlords.

Ground 8

"Both at the date of the service of the notice under section 8 of this Act relating to proceedings for possession and at the date of the hearing:

(a) If rent is payable weekly or fortnightly, at least thirteen weeks rent is unpaid;

(b) If rent is payable monthly, at least three months' rent is unpaid;

(c) If rent is paid quarterly, at least one quarter's rent is more than three months in arrears; and

(d) If rent is payable yearly, at least three months' rent is more than three months in arrears;

and for the purposes of this ground 'rent' means rent lawfully due from the tenant."

This Ground underwent considerable amendment during its passage through the House of Commons.

Its original wording was:

"Both at the date of service of the notice under section 8 of this Act relating to the proceedings for possession and at the date of the hearing, some rent lawfully due from the tenant is more than three months in arrear."

For "some rent" however small has now been substituted thirteen weeks or three months. If the requisite arrears of lawfully due rent are unpaid on both dates the court has no discretion: it must make an order for possession.

Equally if the defendant has paid off the arrears or paid off sufficient of the arrears to bring himself outside the provisions of Ground 8 the court has no discretion and must dismiss the application for possession under this Ground. However the landlord may be entitled to possession under Ground 10 or 11.

Discretionary grounds of possession

The difference between the grounds for possession in Part I and those in Part II is that whilst in the former it is sufficient for the Court to be satisfied that a particular ground is made out, in the latter an order can only be made if the court is also satisfied that it is reasonable to make the order.

Reasonableness

The material time at which the question of reasonableness has to be considered is the date of the trial. The court is required to take all material circumstances into account. This will include every matter which affects either the landlord or the tenant in the dwelling-house as well as the interests of the public at large.

What the court must not do is to ascertain whether or not the landlord's wish to obtain possession is reasonable. Its task is to consider solely whether it is reasonable to make the order for possession if otherwise satisfied that the ground has been established.

The conduct of the parties must be looked at and this includes the conduct of an agent of the landlord. Lack of candour in court may be a factor to be placed on the scales. If a landlord has accepted rent with knowledge of a breach by the tenant of his obligations this may be relevant. The court should consider the length of time that the tenant has resided in the dwelling-house.

In *Creswell* v. *Hodgson* [1951] 1 KB 92 the Court of Appeal held that a judge had not erred in taking into account the fact that the landlord had intended to sell the dwelling-house with vacant possession if he got his order.

Sexual morality of the tenant may be relevant as may be his conduct. If for example a tenant is abusive or offensive that conduct may be material.

Where on the proper interpretation of the 1988 Act certain matters are excluded from consideration in respect of a particular ground of possession such matters do not fall for consideration on the issue of reasonableness.

Ground 9

"Suitable alternative accommodation is available for the tenant or will be available for him when the order for possession takes effect."

Part III of Schedule 2
Suitable alternative accommodation

"1. For the purposes of Ground 9 above, a certificate of the local housing authority for the district in which the dwelling-house in question is situated, certifying that the authority will provide suitable alternative accommodation for the tenant by a date specified in the certificate, shall be conclusive evidence that suitable alternative accommodation will be available for him by that date.

2. Where no such certificate as is mentioned in paragraph 1 above is produced to the court, accommodation shall be deemed to be suitable for the purposes of Ground 9 above if it consists of either:

    (a) premises which are to be let as a separate dwelling such that they will then be let on an assured tenancy, other than:
        (i) a tenancy in respect of which notice is given not later than the beginning of the tenancy that possession might be recovered on any of Grounds 1 to 5 above, or
        (ii) an assured shorthold tenancy, within the meaning of Chapter II of Part I of this Act, or
    (b) premises to be let as a separate dwelling on terms which will, in the opinion of the court, afford to the tenant security of tenure reasonably equivalent to the security afforded by Chapter 1 of Part I of this Act in the case of an assured tenancy of a kind mentioned in sub-paragraph (a) above,

and, in the opinion of the court, the accommodation fulfils the relevant conditions as defined in paragraph 3 below.

3. (1) For the purposes of paragraph 2 above, the relevant conditions are that the accommodation is reasonably suitable to the needs of the tenant and his family as regards proximity to place of work, and either:
    (a) similar as regards rental and extent to the accommodation afforded by the dwelling-houses provided in the neighbourhood by any local housing authority for persons whose needs as regards extent are, in the opinion of the court, similar to those of the tenant and of his family; or
    (b) reasonably suitable to the means of the tenant and to the needs of the tenant and his family as regards extent and character; and
    that if any furniture was provided for use under the assured tenancy in question, furniture is provided for use in the accommodation which is either similar to that so provided

or is reasonably suitable to the needs of the tenant and his family.

(2) For the purposes of sub-paragraph (1)(a) above a certificate of a local housing authority stating:

(a) the extent of the accommodation afforded by dwelling-houses provided by the authority to meet the needs of tenants with families of such number as may be specified in the certificate, and

(b) the amount of the rent charged by the authority for dwelling-houses affording accommodation of that extent, shall be conclusive evidence of the facts so stated.

4. Accommodation shall not be deemed to be suitable to the needs of the tenant and his family if the result of their occupation of the accommodation would be that it would be an overcrowded dwelling-house for the purposes of Part X of the Housing Act 1985.

5. Any document purporting to be a certificate of a local housing authority named therein issued for the purposes of this Part of this Schedule and to be signed by the proper officer of that authority shall be received in evidence and, unless the contrary is shown, shall be deemed to be such a certificate without further proof.

6. In this Part of this Schedule "local housing authority" and "district" in relation to such an authority, have the same meaning as in the Housing Act 1985."

This wording is different from that in section 30(1)(c) of the 1954 Act but it is identical to that in section 98(1) of the 1977 Act. Further the provisions of Part III of Schedule 2 to the 1988 Act as to suitable accommodation are, mutatis mutandis, essentially identical to the provisions of Part IV of the 1977 Act as amended by the 1988 Act, the Housing (Consequential Provisions) Act 1985, the 1985 Act and the 1986 Act.

Thus many decided cases under the Rent Acts will be relevant on this Ground.

In *Gladyric* v. *Collinson* (1983) 267 Estates Gazette 761 C. A. Lawton L.J. at p. 762 said:

"It was pointed out to Mr. Miller in the course of argument that county court judges dealing with this kind of case cannot be expected to give long detailed judgments. Indeed it would not be in the interests of the administration of justice in the county court if they did. They have to get to the heart of the case as quickly as they can and make their findings on it. The heart of this case was whether or not the alternative accommodation which had been offered was suitable. The best way for a county court judge to decide whether it is or it is not is to listen to the evidence of the parties and have a view and having had a view, he is in a far better position than this court to decide whether the offered accommodation is suitable."

Ground 10

"Some rent lawfully due from the tenant:
  (a) is unpaid on the date on which proceedings for possession are begun; and
  (b) except where subsection (1)(b) of section 8 of this Act applies, was in arrears at the date of service of the notice under that section relating to those proceedings."

This Ground is to be contrasted with Ground 8 where no question of reasonableness arises and Ground 11. There are four distinct relevant times. (1) The date at which rent becomes payable. (2) The date on which the notice required to be given by the landlord under section 8 is served. (3) The date on which the landlord commences his proceedings and (4) the date of hearing.

Ground 8 is primarily concerned with (1) and (4). Ground 10 is primarily concerned with (1), (2) and (3), whilst Ground 11 is concerned primarily with (1).

However as regards Ground 10 if under section (8)(1)(b) the court dispenses with the need of a notice then only (1) and (3) will be relevant.

Ground 11

"Whether or not any rent is in arrears on the date on which proceedings for possession are begun, the tenant has persistently delayed paying rent which has become lawfully due."

As the Bill was originally drawn this was one of the Part I Grounds. With its transfer to Part II the court must be satisfied that it is reasonable to make the order.

Ground 12

"Any obligation of the tenancy (other than one relating to the payment of rent) has been broken or not performed."

This wording is to be contrasted with that of section 30(1)(c) of the 1954 Act "other substantial breaches by him of his obligations under the current tenancy or for any other reason connected with the tenant's use or management of the holding".

(a) and (b) of section 30(1) dealt with breach of repairing obligations and persistent delay in paying rent respectively.

The absence of the word "substantial" in Ground 12 will be balanced by the reasonableness requirement.

Any breach of an express or even an implied obligation will be sufficient. If for example the tenant is obliged not to sub-let a sufficient breach will be established by an unlawful sub-letting.

Ground 13

"The condition of dwelling-house or any of the common parts has deteriorated owing to acts of waste by, or the neglect or default of, the tenant or any other person residing in the dwelling-house and, in the case of an act of waste by, or the neglect or default of, a person lodging with the tenant or a sub-tenant of his, the tenant has not taken such steps as he ought reasonably to have taken for the removal of the lodger or sub-tenant.

For the purposes of this ground, "common parts" means any part of a building comprising the dwelling-house and any other premises which the tenant is entitled under the terms of the tenancy to use in common with the occupiers of other dwelling-houses in which the landlord has an estate or interest."

This corresponds in part with Case 3 of Schedule 15 to the 1977 Act.

Here, however, it is not only the condition of the dwelling-house that has to be considered; it also extends to the "common parts" as defined above.

No doubt both under the 1977 Act and this Act a separate case or ground for waste is included since waste, neglect or default does not always amount to a breach of the tenant's obligation under the tenancy.

Ground 14

"The tenant or any other person residing in the dwelling-house has been guilty of conduct which is a nuisance or annoyance to adjoining occupiers, or has been convicted of using the dwelling-house or allowing the dwelling-house to be used for immoral or illegal purposes."

This essentially follows the provisions of Case 2 in Part I of Schedule 15 to the 1977 Act.

Nuisance or Annoyance

This is a question of fact to be determined by a judge on the evidence called before him including inferences to be drawn from such evidence.

It was held by the Court of Appeal in *Cobstone Investments Limited* v. *Maxim* [1984] 3 WLR 563 that "adjoining" is used not in the sense of being immediately contiguous but in the wide sense of neighbourhood. The adjoining occupiers must however be sufficiently close to the dwelling-house of the tenant to be affected by his conduct. Relevant nuisance means an interference with the ordinary comfort of adjoining occupiers, whereas annoyance is a wider definition embracing all matters likely to be a source of trouble in any way to ordinary sensible persons. There need not be physical interference.

Illegal User

Proof of a conviction of a crime committed in the dwelling-house and for which the premises were used is sufficient. Thus handling stolen goods on the premises would be enough. Sustained illegal user does not have to be established but it will be for the judge to decide whether a single conviction is sufficient.

Immoral User

It will not be sufficient for the landlord to establish that unmarried people were living as man and wife. A conviction that the premises were used as a brothel would be cogent evidence of immoral user and not only of illegal user. If a landlord establishes that to the knowledge of the tenant the dwelling-house has been used as a brothel but no criminal proceedings leading to a conviction had been taken a court could be satisfied of immoral user but an easier avenue for a landlord may be on a nuisance or annoyance basis.

Ground 15

"The condition of any furniture provided for use under the tenancy has, in the opinion of the court, deteriorated owing to ill-treatment by the tenant or any other person residing in the dwelling-house and, in the case of ill-treatment by a person lodging with a tenant or by a sub-tenant of his, the tenant has not taken such steps as he ought reasonably to have taken for the removal of the lodger or his sub-tenant."

These provisions mirror Case 4 of Part I of Schedule 15 to the 1977 Act.

Because of the impact of the Business Expansion Scheme, as to which see later, it is probable that the majority of fixed terms and periodic tenancies will contain a term that the tenant must not sub-let or part with possession of the whole or any part of the dwelling-house.

In the case of a periodic tenancy which is silent one way or the other about sub-letting and the like and no premium has been paid there is by virtue of section 15 of the Act an implied term that except with the consent of the landlord, the tenant shall not assign sub-let or part with the possession in whole or in part of the premises. Further by subsection (2) it is provided that section 19 of the Landlord and Tenant Act 1927 (Provisions as to covenants not to assign without licence or consent made subject to a provision to the effect that such licence or consent is not to be unreasonably withheld) shall not apply to such an implied term.

Ground 16

"The dwelling-house was let to the tenant in consequence of his employment by the landlord seeking possession or a previous landlord under the tenancy and the tenant has ceased to be in that employment."

There are no similar provisions in the 1977 Act.

Chapter 8

Notices in Respect of Assured Tenancies

(a) Notices of proceedings for possession

Section 8 deals with notices which a landlord must serve if he wishes to recover possession.

The prescribed notices are printed in Appendix A.

The notice served by the landlord or in the case of joint landlords by at least one of them must inform the tenant that:

(a) he intends to begin proceedings for possession of the dwelling-house on one or more of the grounds specified in the notice (which of course must be a ground in Part I or II of Schedule 2);

(b) the proceedings will not begin earlier than a date specified in the notice which, without prejudice to any additional limitation, as to which see below, shall not be earlier than the expiry of the period of two weeks from the date of the notice; and

(c) those proceedings will not begin later than 12 months from the date of service of the notice.

The additional limitation arises when one of the grounds for possession (whether with or without other grounds) is Ground 1, 2, 5, 6, 7, 9 or 16 in Schedule 2.

Then the earliest date which may be stated in the notice is two months from its date.

A further limitation arises in the case of a periodic tenancy. The date specified cannot be earlier than the earliest date on which the tenancy could be brought to an end by a notice to quit given by the landlord on the same date as the date of the service of the notice.

If, however, the periodic tenancy contains powers for the landlord to determine a tenancy in certain circumstances and the landlord exercises that power the last limitation does not apply.

Provision is made in the case of notices where the tenancy is for a fixed term.

In advance of the expiry of such a tenancy by effluxion of time and the coming into being of a statutory periodic tenancy a notice

may be served so long as the date specified is after the coming
to an end of the fixed term, unless of course the landlord having
power to do so has exercised his power to determine the tenancy
at an earlier date.

The notice is also effective if the ground or grounds specified
relate/s to events which occurred during a fixed term tenancy notwithstanding that the tenancy has become a statutory periodic
tenancy.

Power is given to the court to dispense with the requirements
of the notice when it is just and equitable to do so. It would seem
likely that very compelling circumstances would have to exist before
a court would be justified in dispensing with the need for a notice.

That power in any event can never be exercised where a landlord
is seeking to recover possession for non-payment of rent as provided
for in ground 8.

(b) Notices that may be given in respect of Grounds 1 to 5.

As has been seen Grounds 1, 2, 3, 4 and 5 make provision for
the giving of a notice in writing by a landlord. Part IV of Schedule
2 sets out the additional provisions relating to such a notice.

Where there are joint landlords a notice by one at least is sufficient.
Where there are immediately successive tenants of substantially the
same dwelling-house then a valid notice in writing given at the commencement of the first tenancy applies equally to later tenancies.

But a landlord may exclude the operation of that provision by
giving a further notice at the commencement of the later tenancy
that it is not one in respect of which possession can be recovered
on the ground in question.

There are certain minor consequential provisions:

First so far as Ground 1 is concerned the reference in paragraph
(b) thereof to the reversion on the tenancy is both a reference to
the reversion on the earlier tenancy and to that of any relevant
later tenancy.

Secondly so far as Ground 3 or 4 is concerned any second or
subsequent tenancy in relation to which the notice has effect shall
be treated for the purposes of that ground as beginning at the beginning
of the tenancy in respect of which the notice was actually given.

Thirdly any reference in Grounds 1 to 5 to a notice being given
not later than the beginning of the tenancy is a reference to its
being given not later than the day on which the tenancy is entered
into.

Thus the provisions of section 45(2) do not apply.

Section 45(2) provides "Subject to paragraph 11 of Schedule 2 to this Act, any reference in this part of the Act to the beginning of a tenancy is a reference to the day on which, under the terms of any lease, agreement or other document, the tenant is entitled to possession under the tenancy".

Chapter 9

Court Proceedings

(a) Court Jurisdiction

Section 40 makes provision for the courts which are to have jurisdiction to hear and determine any question inter alia under the various provisions of the Act relating to assured tenancies.

The provisions are not dissimilar to those in section 141 of the 1977 Act.

The section operates to confer on the county court an unlimited jurisdiction in respect of an assured tenancy which extends beyond the normal limits of county court jurisdiction. The normal limits are £5,000 for the recovery of rent and a rateable value of £1,000 for the recovery of land.

But it is not an exclusive jurisdiction. A landlord may, however, be ill-advised to bring his proceedings in the High Court by virtue of the provisions of sub-section (4). This provides that if any person takes any proceedings under any of the provisions of the Act relating to assured tenancies he shall not be entitled to recover any more costs for those proceedings than those to which he would have been entitled if the proceedings had been taken in the county court: and in any such case the Taxing Master shall have the same power of directing on what county court scale costs are to be allowed and of allowing any item of cost, as the judge would have had if the proceedings had been taken in the county court.

However those provisions do not apply where the landlord's purpose of taking proceedings in the High Court is to enable them to be joined with proceedings already pending before the court (not being proceedings taken under any of the relevant provisions relating to assured tenancies in this Act).

Where the county court is exercising jurisdiction in relation to proceedings in respect of an assured tenancy the court also has jurisdiction to hear and determine any other proceedings joined with those proceedings, notwithstanding that, without this conferral of jurisdiction, those other proceedings would be outside the court's jurisdiction.

Neither the High Court nor the county court has jurisdiction in respect of any question which falls within the jurisdiction of a rent assessment committee by virtue of any of the relevant provisions of the Act.

(b) Requirement as to court orders and powers of the court

Unless there is a surrender or other action by the tenant the landlord can only obtain possession consequent upon a court order in possession proceedings initiated by him.

Section 9 gives the court wide powers in possession cases relating to assured tenancies in certain circumstances.

These powers, however, do not arise where a mandatory ground for possession is established by a landlord under Part I of Schedule 2.

By sub-section (1) the court may adjourn proceedings for possession for such period or periods as it thinks fit.

On the making of an order for possession or at any time before the execution of such an order the court may (a) stay or suspend execution of the order or (b) postpone the date of possession, for such period or periods as the court thinks just.

However if the court does so adjourn, stay, suspend or postpone the court is required, unless it considers that to do so would cause exceptional hardship to the tenant or would otherwise be unreasonable, to impose conditions with regard to payment by the tenant of arrears of rent (if any) and rent or payment in respect of rent or mesne profits (payments in respect of occupation after the termination of the tenancy) and may impose such other conditions as it thinks fit.

Where such conditions are imposed but they are complied with the court may then, if it thinks fit, discharge or rescind any order previously made or stay or suspend the execution of an order for possession or postpone the date of possession.

Provision is made for a spouse or former spouse having rights of occupation under the Matrimonial Homes Act 1983.

By this Act where one spouse has a right to remain in occupation of a dwelling-house and the other spouse has no such right, the latter is given protection against eviction or exclusion from the dwelling-house by the other spouse except with the leave of the court and if not in occupation, is given a right, with the leave of the court to occupy the dwelling-house. The Act does not apply to a dwelling-house which has at no time been a matrimonial home and, except as provided in section 2, the protection which the Act gives continues only so long as the marriage subsists.

The Act applies as between a husband and a wife notwithstanding that the marriage in question was entered into under a law which permits polygamy (whether or not either party to the marriage in question has for the time being a spouse additional to the other party).

If at the time proceedings are brought for possession the dwelling-house is let on an assured tenancy and the assured tenancy is terminated as a result of those proceedings, the spouse or the former spouse so long as he or she remains in occupation has the same rights in relation to or in connection with any adjournment as is referred to in section 9(1) or any stay, suspension or postponement as is referred to in section 9(2) as he or she would have if those rights of occupation were not affected by the termination of the tenancy.

Chapter 10

Assured Shorthold Tenancies

The 1980 Act introduced the notion of a "protected shorthold tenancy" which is defined in section 52(1)(a),(b),(c) as a "protected tenancy granted after the commencement of this section which is granted for a term certain of not less than one year nor more than five years and satisfies the following conditions:

(a) it cannot be brought to an end by the landlord before the expiry of the term, except in pursuance of a provision for re-entry or forfeiture for non-payment of rent or breach of any other obligation of the tenancy; and

(b) before the grant the landlord has given the tenant a valid notice stating that the tenancy is to be a protected shorthold tenancy; and

(c) either a rent for the dwelling-house is registered at the time the tenancy is granted. . . ."

In the case of s52(1)(c) where there is no registered rent two conditions must be fulfilled:

(i) an application for a registered rent must be made within twenty-eight days of the grant of the tenancy, and

(ii) before this determination the rent must not exceed the amount specified in a certificate of fair rent.

However, the Protected Shorthold Tenancies (Rent Registration) Order 1987 (SI 1987 No 265) has removed the requirement of section 52(1)(c) generally.

A protected shorthold tenancy may be brought to an end (notwithstanding any contrary agreed terms) before the expiry of the term certain by notice in writing given by the tenant to the landlord. Such length of notice must, under s53(1), be:

(a) one month if the term certain is two years or less; and

(b) three months if it is more than two years.

Case 19 of Schedule 15 to the 1977 Act is a special mandatory ground of possession for the protected shorthold tenancy. Possession will be obtained if the dwelling-house was let under a protected shorthold tenancy and

73

(a) there either has been no grant of a further tenancy of the dwelling-house since the end of the protected shorthold tenancy or, if there was such a grant, it was to a person who immediately before the grant was in possession of the dwelling-house as a protected or statutory tenant; and

(b) the proceedings were commenced after appropriate notice to the tenant and not later than three months after the expiry of the notice.

Qualifying conditions for assured shorthold tenancies

The 1988 Act introduces a new form of tenancy entitled an assured shorthold tenancy which is a variant of an assured tenancy under the 1988 Act. The assured shorthold tenancy provides the landlord with a facility for repossessing the demised premises at the end of the term. The tenancy also allows the tenant to refer the question of the rent payable under the assured shorthold tenancy to a rent assessment committee if the tenant considers that the rent payable is significantly in excess of the rents payable under either assured tenancies or assured shorthold tenancies under the 1988 Act. A tenancy is an assured shorthold tenancy if the following conditions are met namely:

(a) it is granted for a term certain of not less than six months and

(b) a notice is served which is one which:
  (i) is in such form as may be prescribed;
  (ii) is served before the assured tenancy is entered into;
  (iii) is served by the person who is to be the landlord under the assured tenancy on the person who is to be the tenant under that tenancy; and
  (iv) states that the assured tenancy to which it relates is to be a shorthold tenancy.

Notices prescribed in respect of assured shorthold tenancies are in Appendix A.

There is a saving provision in section 20(4) of the 1988 Act to the effect that on the coming to an end of an assured shorthold tenancy, if a new assured tenancy of the same or substantially the same premises comes into being under which the landlord and tenant are the same as at the coming to an end of the earlier tenancy, the new tenancy is deemed to be an assured shorthold tenancy whether or not it fulfills the conditions in (a) and (b) above.

Tenancies which cannot be assured shorthold tenancies

A tenancy cannot be an assured shorthold tenancy where immediately before the new tenancy was granted the person to whom it was granted was a tenant under an assured tenancy which was not a shorthold tenancy and was granted by the landlord under the assured tenancy; section 20(3)(a),(b) of the 1988 Act. A further exclusion is contained in section 20(5) of the 1988 Act whereby the saving provision in section 20(4) (explained above) does not apply if, before the new assured tenancy is entered into, the landlord serves notice on the tenant that the new tenancy was not to be a shorthold tenancy. The same exclusion applies where instead of the notice being served before the new assured tenancy is entered into it is served before a statutory periodic tenancy takes effect in possession.

Rent under an assured shorthold tenancy

In general, the same rules apply to the determination of the rent, by a rent assessment committee, under an assured shorthold tenancy as in the case of an assured tenancy; section 20(7) of the 1988 Act. The rent assessment committee has two functions in the case of an assured shorthold tenancy namely (a) the determination of the rent following a notice served by the landlord proposing an increase in rent and (b) the determination of the rent where the tenant considers that the rent payable under the tenancy is significantly higher than the rents payable under assured or assured shorthold tenancies of similar dwelling-houses in the locality.

If a tenant under an assured shorthold tenancy has received a notice proposing a new rent which satisfies section 13(2) of the 1988 Act an assured shorthold tenant may refer the notice to a rent assessment committee. The rent assessment committee is to determine the rent at which it considers that the dwelling-house concerned might reasonably be expected to let in the open market by a willing landlord under an assured shorthold tenancy; section 14(1). See generally Chapter 5 as to notices and powers of a rent assessment committee.

Reference of excessive rent to rent assessment committee

Under the 1988 Act, if a tenant under an assured shorthold tenancy which satisfies the qualifying conditions outlined in section 20 of that Act considers that the rent payable under the tenancy is significantly higher than the rents payable under assured tenancies or assured shorthold tenancies of similar dwelling-houses in the locality, he may make an application to the rent assessment committee for the determination of the rent which, in the committee's opinion, the landlord might reasonably be expected to obtain under the assured shorthold tenancy; section 22(1) of the 1988 Act. The prescribed form is in Appendix D. There appear to be several problem areas in the interpretation of these provisions, in particular (i) there is no definition of the term "significantly higher" although it may be that this would be substantial; (ii) the "locality" is not defined but some guidance may be obtained from the authorities on the interpretation of section 70 of the 1977 Act.

If the rent assessment committee makes a determination under section 22 of the 1988 Act its determination takes effect from such date as it may direct but this date cannot be earlier than the date of the application. In addition, if at any time on or after the determination takes effect the rent which would be payable under the tenancy exceeds the rent so determined the excess is irrecoverable from the tenant; s22(4)(b) of the 1988 Act. There is a limit placed upon the date of service of a notice to increase the rent under section 13(2) as no such notice may be served in respect of the assured shorthold tenancy of the dwelling-house in question until after the first anniversary of the date on which the determination by the rent assessment committee under section 22 takes place. Under section 22(3)(a),(b) the rent assessment committee cannot make a determination unless there is a sufficient number of similar dwelling-houses in the locality let on assured tenancies or assured shorthold tenancies and that the rent payable under the assured shorthold tenancy in question is significantly higher than the rent which the landlord might reasonably be expected to be able to obtain under the tenancy having regard to the level of rents payable under the tenancies. It appears as a matter of construction that the disregards in section 14(2) of the 1988 Act do not apply to the matters under section 22.

Restrictions on the right to refer

It is not possible to refer the matter of the excessive rent to a rent assessment committee in every case. No application may be made for the determination of the rent payable, for example, if the rent payable under the tenancy is a rent previously determined under section 22. The saving provision in section 20(4) of the 1988 Act is also applicable in this context because it provides that on the coming to an end of an assured shorthold tenancy, if a new assured tenancy of the same or substantially the same premises comes into being under which the landlord and tenant are the same as at the coming to an end of the earlier tenancy, the new tenancy is deemed to be an assured shorthold tenancy whether or not it fulfils the conditions in (a) and (b) above. In such a case no application may be made for a determination.

Recovery of possession on expiry or termination

A landlord under an assured shorthold tenancy can recover possession either under the provisions of sections 5–12 and Schedule 2 to the 1988 Act or under the provisions of section 21. The application of sections 5–12 and Schedule 2 of the 1988 Act are dealt with in detail in Chapter 7. Under section 21 on or after the coming to an end of a fixed term assured shorthold tenancy a court must make an order for possession if it is satisfied (section 21(1)(a),(b)):

> "(a) that the assured shorthold tenancy has come to an end and no further assured tenancy (whether shorthold or not) is for the time being in existence, other than a statutory periodic tenancy; and
>
> (b) the landlord or, in the case of joint landlords, at least one of them has given to the tenant not less than two months' notice stating that he requires possession of the dwelling-house."

The notice referred to in section 21(1)(b) may be given before or on the day on which the tenancy comes to an end and notwithstanding that on the coming to an end of the fixed term tenancy a statutory periodic tenancy arises. If the court makes an order for possession of a dwelling-house under section 21 of the 1988 Act any statutory periodic tenancy which has arisen on the coming to an end of the assured shorthold tenancy ends on the day on which the order takes effect. Finally, under section 21(4)(a),(b) there are provisions for dealing with the case of a *periodic* assured shorthold tenancy. In such a case the court must make an order for possession if it is satisfied that the landlord has given to the tenant a notice stating that, after a date specified in the notice (which must not be earlier than the earliest day on which the tenancy could be brought to an end by a notice to quit given by the landlord on the same day as that notice), which is to be (i) the last day of the period of the tenancy and (ii) not earlier than two months after the date the notice was given, possession of the dwelling-house is required.

Effect of re-entry provisions

Section 20 of the 1988 Act reads "(1) ... an assured shorthold tenancy is an assured tenancy ... (b) in respect of which there is no power for the landlord to determine the tenancy at any time earlier than six months from the beginning of the tenancy".

These words are to be contrasted with the very different words appearing in section 52(1)(a) of the 1980 Act set out on page 73. It is the absence in section 20(1)(b) of the words "except in pursuance of a provision for re-entry for forfeiture for non-payment of rent or breach of any other obligation of the tenancy" which, if literally interpreted may cause considerable problems.

Section 52 is concerned with the bringing to an end of a tenancy whereas section 20(1)(b) relates to the power to determine the tenancy. It seems that it is unlikely that the two differ in any relevant respects. It may therefore be that it will be necessary so to draft the forfeiture clause in the assured shorthold tenancy agreement that it does not operate in the first six months.

Chapter 11

Assured Agricultural Occupancies

A modified form of assured tenancy is introduced by Part III of the 1988 Act in the form of assured agricultural occupancies which is defined in section 24(1) of that Act as being a "tenancy or licence of a dwelling house" which (a) complies with the qualifying conditions outlined in section 24(1)(a) and (b) which, by virtue of any provision of Schedule 3 of the Act, the agricultural worker condition is for the time being fulfilled with respect to the dwelling-house subject to the tenancy or licence. A tenancy or license for the purpose of section 24(1)(a) or (b) is either (a) an assured tenancy which is not an assured shorthold tenancy or (b) a tenancy which is not an assured tenancy merely by reason of being excluded by paragraphs 3 (tenancies at low rent) or 7 (tenancies of agricultural holdings) in Schedule 1 to the 1988 Act or (c) a licence under which a person has exclusive possession of a dwelling-house as a separate dwelling and which, if it conferred a sufficient interest in land, would be a tenancy satisfying the tests in (a) and (b) (above).

Agricultural worker condition

For the agreement to form an assured agricultural occupancy not only must the agreement amount to a "tenancy" or "licence" within the meaning of section 24(1)(a), 2(a)(b)(c) of the 1988 Act but also the agricultural worker condition must be satisfied with respect to such a tenancy or licence. The qualifying conditions to satisfy the agricultural worker condition are contained in Schedule 3 to the 1988 Act which itself refers to Schedule 3 to the Rent (Agriculture) Act 1976 for determining the following, namely:

(a) whether a person is a qualifying worker;
(b) whether a person is incapable of whole-time work in agriculture, or work in agriculture as a permit worker, in consequence of a qualifying injury or disease; and
(c) whether a dwelling-house is in qualifying ownership.

By virtue of Schedule 3 to the 1988 Act the agricultural worker condition is satisfied with respect to a dwelling-house subject to a relevant tenancy or licence if (para 2):

79

  (a) the dwelling-house is or has been in qualifying ownership
      at any time during the subsistence of the tenancy or licence
      (whether or not it was at that time a relevant tenancy or
      licence); and
  (b) the occupier or, where there are joint occupiers, at least
      one of them:
      (i) is a qualifying worker or has been a qualifying worker
          at any time during the subsistence of the tenancy or
          licence (whether or not it was at that time a relevant
          tenancy or licence); or
      (ii) is incapable of whole-time work in agriculture or work
           in agriculture as a permit worker in consequence of
           a qualifying injury or disease.

At this stage it is useful to note the definitions of "qualifying
ownership", "qualifying worker" and "incapable of whole-time
work in agriculture" contained in Schedule 3 to the Rent (Agriculture) Act 1976. In general the definitions to be applied are as follows,
although the reader should refer to the whole of Schedule 3 to
the 1976 Act to satisfy himself that the conditions are satisfied:

Qualifying worker

1. A person is a qualifying worker for the purposes of this Act
at any time if, at that time, he has worked whole-time in agriculture,
or has worked in agriculture as a permit worker, for not less than
91 out of the last 104 weeks.

Incapable of whole-time work in agriculture, or work in agriculture as a permit worker, in consequence of a qualifying injury or disease

2.—(1) A person is, for the purposes of this Act, incapable of
whole-time work in agriculture in consequence of a qualifying injury
or disease if:

  (a) he is incapable of such work in consequence of:
      (i) an injury or disease prescribed in relation to him, by
          reason of his employment in agriculture, under section
          76(2) of the Social Security Act 1975, or
      (ii) an injury caused by an accident arising out of and in
           the course of his employment in agriculture, and
  (b) at the time when he became so incapable, he was employed
      in agriculture as a whole-time worker.

(2) A person is, for the purposes of this Act, incapable of work
in agriculture as a permit worker in consequence of a qualifying
injury or disease if:

(a) he is incapable of such work in consequence of any such injury or disease as is mentioned in sub-paragraph (1) above,
   and

(b) at the time when he became so incapable he was employed
   in agriculture as a permit worker.

(3) Where:

(a) A person has died in consequence of any such injury or
   disease as is mentioned in sub-paragraph (1) above, and

(b) immediately before his death, he was employed in agriculture as a whole-time worker, or as a permit worker,

he shall be regarded for the purposes of this Act as having been,
immediately before his death, incapable of whole-time work in agriculture, or work in agriculture as a permit worker, in consequence
of a qualifying injury or disease.

Dwelling-house in qualifying ownership

3.(1) A dwelling-house in relation to which a person ("the occupier") has a licence or tenancy is in qualifying ownership for the
purposes of this Act at any time if, at that time, the occupier is
employed in agriculture and the occupier's employer either:

(a) is the owner of the dwelling-house, or

(b) has made arrangements with the owner of the dwelling-
   house for it to be used as housing accommodation for persons employed by him in agriculture.

There are provisions for satisfying the agricultural worker conditions where the qualifying worker is deceased and immediately
before his death the widow or widower was residing in the dwelling-
house (para 3(1)(b)(2) of Schedule 3) or in the case of succession
by the qualifying member of the previous qualifying occupier's
family (namely not the widow or widower), such a member of the
family is the qualifying member of the family if:

(a) on the death of the previous qualifying occupier there was
   no qualifying widow or widower, and

(b) the member of the family was residing in the dwelling-house
   with the previous qualifying occupier at the time of, and
   for the period of two years before his death.

Determination of rent by rent assessment committee

By virtue of section 24(4) of the 1988 Act the provisions of section
14 as to the determination of rent by a rent assessment committee
are applied to assured agricultural occupancies. The reader should

refer to Chapter 5 at page 33 for a full analysis of the provisions as to rent and other terms. It is to be noted that under section 24(3) of the 1988 Act every assured agricultural occupancy which is not an assured tenancy is to be treated as if it were such a tenancy subject to the provisions of sections 24 to 26 of the 1988 Act.

Security of tenure

The security of tenure provisions applicable to assured agricultural occupancies are contained in section 25 to Schedule 2 of the 1988 Act. If a statutory periodic tenancy arises on the coming to an end of an assured agicultural occupancy it is an assured agricultural occupancy as long as, under Schedule 3, the agricultural worker condition is for the time being fulfilled and, if no rent was payable under the assured agricultural occupancy, the provisions of section 5(3)(d) are to be read as if the rent under the periodic tenancy was a monthly one; section 25(1)(b) of the 1988 Act. The grounds of posession are as contained in Part II of Schedule 2 to the 1988 Act save that Ground 16 is not available against the tenant or licensee under the assured agricultural occupancy. However, it is to be noted that Part III of Schedule 2, dealing with the provision of suitable alternative accommodation, is applicable. If the tenant under an agreed agricultural occupancy gives notice to terminate his employment then, notwithstanding anything in any agreement or otherwise, that notice does not constitute a notice to quit as respects the assured agricultural occupancy; section 25(5) of the 1988 Act. Finally, there are provisions in section 27 of the Rent (Agriculture) Act 1976 for rehousing agricultural workers by local housing authorities where:

(a) vacant possession is or will be needed of a dwelling-house which is subject to a protected occupancy or statutory tenancy, or which is let subject to a tenancy to which subsection (1) applies, in order to house a person who is or is to be employed in agriculture by the applicant, and that person's family,

(b) the applicant is unable to provide, by any reasonable means, suitable alternative accommodation for the occupier of the dwelling-house, and

(c) the authority ought, in the interests of efficient agriculture, to provide the suitable alternative accommodation.

These provisions are applied to assured agricultural occupancies by virtue of section 26 of the 1988 Act.

For the prescribed forms see Appendix A.

Chapter 12

Miscellaneous Provisions

(a) Provisions as to reversion—assured tenancies

Where a dwelling-house is lawfully let on an assured tenancy and the landlord is himself a tenant under a superior tenancy which ends, the assured tenancy nevertheless continues as a tenancy held of the person whose interest would, apart from such continuance entitle him to actual possession of the dwelling-house at that time.

But these provisions do not apply when by virtue of the application of Schedule 1 the landlord's interest would result in the tenancy not being an assured one.

Provision is also made for the position where an assured periodic tenancy (including a statutory periodic tenancy) continues beyond the beginning of the tenancy which was granted whether before or after the commencement of the Act, so as to begin on or after the date on which the fixed term tenancy came to an end (being then followed by a statutory periodic tenancy) or a date on which, apart from the 1988 Act, a periodic tenancy could have been brought to an end by the landlord by a notice to quit. The reversionary tenancy is to have effect as though it had been granted subject to the periodic tenancy. See generally section 18.

(b) Access for repairs

Section 16 provides that it shall be an implied term of every assured tenancy that the tenant shall afford to the landlord access to the dwelling-house let on the tenancy and all reasonable facilities for executing on the premises any repairs which the landlord is entitled to execute.

(c) Payment of removal expenses in certain cases

Where a landlord recovers possessions on the mandatory ground that he intends to demolish or reconstruct the whole or a substantial part of the building (Ground 6) or on the discretionary ground of offering suitable alternative accommodation (Ground 9) the landlord must pay to the tenant a sum equal to the reasonable expenses likely to be incurred by the tenant in removing from the dwelling-house.

If the parties cannot agree the sum the court must determine it. If not paid the tenant can recover the sum as a civil debt due from the landlord. See generally section 11.

(d) Limited prohibition on assignment

In the case of an assured periodic tenancy a term is implied that the tenant shall not assign the tenancy (in whole or in part) nor sub-let or part with possession of the whole or any part of the dwelling-house without the landlord's consent, section 15(1). In such a case the implied proviso under section 19 of the Landlord and Tenant Act 1927, namely that consent cannot be unreasonably withheld, does not apply; section 15(2).

It is to be noted that the implied term under section 15(1) of the 1988 Act does not apply in the case of a periodic tenancy which is not a statutory periodic tenancy if there is a pro-vision (whether contained in the tenancy or not) prohibiting or permitting (absolutely or conditionally) assigning, subletting or parting with possession or there is a provision requiring a premium to be paid on the grant or renewal of the tenancy: section 15(3)(a),(b).

(e) "Beginning of a tenancy"

Section 45(2) provides that subject to paragraph 11 of Schedule 2 (special provisions regarding a landlord's notice in writing in respect of Grounds 1–5) any reference in sections 1–45 to the begin-ning of a tenancy is a reference to the day on which the tenancy is entered into or, if it is later, the day on which, under the terms of any lease, agreement or other document, the tenant is entitled to possession under the tenancy.

(f) Compensation for misrepresentation or concealment

Section 12 provides that where a landlord obtains an order for possession of a dwelling-house let on an assured tenancy on one or more of the grounds in Schedule 2 and it is subsequently made to appear to the court that the order was obtained by a misrepresen-tation or concealment of material facts that court may order the landlord to pay to the former tenant such sum as appears sufficient as compensation for damage or loss sustained by that tenant as a result of the order.

These provisions are very similar to those contained in section 102 of the Rent Act 1977 and section 55 of the Landlord and Tenant Act 1954. Indeed the provisions in the Rent Acts field has a history which goes back to the Increase of Rent and Mortgage Interest (Restrictions) Act 1920.

They do not apply where the landlord of a fixed term tenancy obtains an order for possession not on one or more of the grounds set out in Schedule 2 but pursuant to the powers in the tenancy exercised by him to determine the tenancy in certain circumstances.

The words "concealment of material facts" as was made clear by Scott L.J. in *Thorne* v. *Smith* 148 Estates Gazette 601 [1947] KB 307, emanate from uberrimae fidei contracts and in these circumstances the standard of conduct demanded of a landlord is utmost good faith. The cause of action afforded by the section is additional to and not in substitution of common law remedies such as an action for deceit; *French* v. *Lowen* (1925) 105 Estates Gazette 491. Both causes of action can be joined in one proceedings. Innocent misrepresentation can be sufficient for the purposes of this section. Damages are compensatory not punitive: *Engleheart* v. *Catford* (1926) 108 Estates Gazette 731 (C.A.).

In practice the damages that will be recoverable may be small. The tenant will have lost a tenancy. Had his former tenancy continued it would of course have been at a market rent and therefore its equity small: see *Clark* v. *Kirby-Smith* 190 Estates Gazette 865 [1964] Ch. 506 (a case on Solicitors' negligence).

(g)   Restriction on levy of distress on rent

These provisions are similar to those contained in section 147(2) of the 1977 Act, where the restrictions imposed by sub-section (1) of that section upon the levy of distress for rent on a protected or statutory tenant do not apply to distress levied under section 102 of the County Courts Act 1984.

Section 19(1) of the 1988 Act provides that subject to the 1984 Act no distress for the rent of any dwelling-house let on an assured tenancy shall be levied except with the leave of the county court.

Where an application is made to the county court for leave to distrain, the county court has the same powers with respect of adjournment, stay, suspension, postponement and otherwise as are conferred on the court by section 9 in relation to proceedings for possession of such a dwelling-house.

(h)   No right to enfranchisement nor right to buy

The provisions of the Leasehold Reform Act 1967 as amended only extend to a house on a long lease that is to say for a term exceeding 21 years at a rent of less than two thirds of the rateable value.

Since no such tenancy whatever its rateable value can be an assured tenancy there will be no right to enfranchisement or to an extended lease.

Under Part I of the Landlord and Tenant Act 1987 a landlord of flat premises is prohibited from disposing of those premises unless he has offered qualifying tenants first refusal to purchase his interest. The provisions apply to premises comprising two or more flats held by qualifying tenants where such flats make up at least half of the flats in the building. Certain tenants are excluded such as protected, shorthold, business or service tenants.

By an amendment of the 1988 Act the classes excluded from such rights were extended to an assured tenancy or an assured agricultural occupancy.

(i)   Repairing obligations in short leases

Important provisions are contained in sections 11–16 of the Landlord and Tenant Act 1985 relating to repairing obligations in respect of certain leases of dwelling-houses where the lease is for less than seven years. In cases where the provisions apply there is implied a covenant by the landlord

(a) to keep in repair the structure and exterior of the dwelling-house (including drains, gutters and external pipes).

(b) to keep in repair and proper working order the installation in the dwelling-house for the supply of water, gas and electricity and for sanitation (including basins, sinks, baths and sanitary conveniences), but not other fixtures, fittings and appliances for making use of the supply of water, gas or electricity and

(c) to keep in repair and proper working order the installations in the dwelling-house for space heating and heating water.

Section 116 of the 1988 Act extends significantly a landlord's obligation in respect of leases granted on or after the 15th January 1989.

These obligations, however, are subject to a number of important qualifications.

The landlord's liability does not extend to works or repairs for which the tenant is liable by reason of his own duty to use the premises in a tenant-like manner or for which the tenant would be liable apart from any express covenant on his part.

As the majority of Mark I assured tenancies were long leases external etc. repairing obligations could be placed on the tenant. In the private sector particularly where a dwelling-house is provided under a Business Expansion Scheme it is likely that these provisions will often apply.

Chapter 13

Business Expansion Scheme

So important are the provisions of the Scheme and their likely affect on assured tenancies that some consideration of the Scheme is essential.

But anyone considering whether to become involved in the Scheme whether directly or indirectly, whether as adviser, or as provider of assured tenancies or as an investor or otherwise is strongly recommended to go to experienced financial advisers.

The inclusion of the relevant sections of the Income and Corporation Taxes Act 1988 (sections 289–312 contained in Chapter III of Part VII) and the Finance Act 1988 (sections 50 & 51) would have added some 50 pages to this book and would have changed its nature. They have therefore been omitted.

But the principal requirements of these provisions are set out in the following pages.

It is important to appreciate that the Scheme does not apply to assured shorthold tenancies as defined in the 1988 Act.

Assured tenancy business expansion schemes are likely to be particularly important because the Finance Act 1988 introduced a ceiling of £500,000 on the total amount of capital raised by most companies in a given period which may qualify for relief under the Scheme.

It is only in respect of assured tenancies and certain ship-chartering companies that the limit does not apply. Instead a very different limit of £5,000,000 is permitted.

The regulations which apply to most BES companies restricting the proportion of their assets which may consist of land or buildings do not apply to assured tenancy companies.

Extension of business expansion schemes to assured tenancies

The Scheme does not in any way extend the definition of an assured tenancy. But it is not every assured tenancy within the 1988 Act which can come within the Scheme. At present investment under the BES can only be made up to the 31st December 1993 in respect of assured tenancies.

A qualifying company

The company must be incorporated in the United Kingdom and be resident only in this country. A very important date is that on which it issues its eligible shares. From that date for a period of four years it must remain resident in the United Kingdom. During that period the company must not be listed on the Stock Exchange and its shares must not be dealt with on the Unlisted Securities Market. However, it may be listed on the Third Market and its shares dealt with there.

It must not be a subsidiary of or be controlled by any other company.

It must carry on qualifying activities or exist to hold all the shares in its subsidiaries which themselves must carry on qualifying activities or be dormant. The company may have layers of subsidiaries which must be at least 90 per cent owned at each level by the parent company. All of its issued share capital must be fully paid up.

Qualifying activities

These activities are defined by section 50 of the Finance Act 1988. These are activities which consist of or are connected with the provision and maintenance of dwelling-houses which the company or its subsidiary lets or intends to let on assured tenancies within the 1988 Act. The company may have a freehold or leasehold interest in the dwelling-house which may be let furnished or unfurnished.

The activities of the company for a period of four years from the date of the issue of the eligible shares must be conducted on a commercial basis and with a view to the realisation of profit.

The company may not make non-qualifying lettings or carry on other non-qualifying activities, such as dealing in land to a substantial extent. Substantial is not defined. In other contexts the Inland Revenue has treated this as more than 20 per cent of turnover.

Qualifying tenancies

These are assured tenancies whether furnished or unfurnished as defined in the 1988 Act subject to the following exceptions:

(a) A tenancy that relates to a dwelling-house which has a market value, on the date that the interest in the property is first acquired (or on the date qualifying shares are issued, if later) greater than £125,000 if the dwelling-house is in

Greater London, or £85,000 if it is elsewhere. [For the meaning of Greater London see Chapter 3 above.]

(b) A tenancy granted in consideration of a premium within the meaning of Schedule 3 to the Capital Gains Tax Act 1979

(c) A tenancy where an option to purchase in relation to the dwelling-house has been granted to the tenant or a joint tenant or an associate of his.

(d) A tenancy of a dwelling-house which is unfit for human habitation within the meaning of section 604 of the Housing Act 1985 or does not have all the standard amenities within the meaning of section 508 of that Act.

(e) A tenancy of a dwelling-house which was already let or in respect of which the company or any subsidiary had entered into arrangements to let before the company or its subsidiary had acquired an interest in that property.

(f) A tenancy of a dwelling-house which has previously qualified as part of another company's qualifying activity.

(g) A tenancy of a dwelling-house in respect of which the company is entitled to capital allowance under Paragraph 2 of Schedule 12 to the Finance Act 1982.

No qualifying tenancy can be entered into until the relevant provisions of the 1988 Act come into force on the 15th January 1989.

As regards (a) certain assumptions are required to be made in determining the market value of a dwelling-house. In the case of a house the assumption is that it is a freehold house with vacant possession; in the case of a flat the assumption is that it is held on a 125 year lease with an annual rent of £10.

A house with a value in excess of the limit may be acquired and then converted for letting so long as the value of each flat does not exceed the limit.

If the value of the property increases so as to take it above the limit such increase will be disregarded if the increase occurs after the relevant date.

If, however, improvements in the course of conversion bring the value of a flat above the limit that flat will be disqualified.

However, if the other flats remain below the limit it would seem that they will not be disqualified.

Certain assumptions as to the state of the premises are required to be made:

(a) that the dwelling-house was in the same state as it is when the valuation is carried. out. Thus any improvements, as mentioned above, will be taken into account even if not in existence at the relevant date; and

(b) that the locality in which the dwelling-house is situated is in the same state at the relevant date as it is when the valuation is made. This means that the valuer looks at other premises in the locality and the occupation and use of those premises together with the transport services and other facilities available in the locality.

Eligible shares

These are shares issued between the 29th July 1988 and 31st December 1993 for the purpose of raising money for qualifying activities. They must be ordinary shares carrying no preferential rights. They must be issued by an unquoted company. They must be new shares. The issued share capital must be fully paid up.

Qualifying individuals

An individual must be resident and ordinarily resident in the United Kingdom within the meaning of the tax legislation at the time when the company shares are issued to him. Certain Crown employees working abroad may be treated as resident and ordinarily resident in the UK for this purpose. He must not be connected with the company or become connected with it within five years of the date of the issue of the shares to him if he wishes to retain the tax relief he obtains.

The principal rules relating to connections with a company are that:

(a) an individual or an associate of his must not be an employee, partner or paid director of the company nor a tenant nor occupier of a dwelling-house in which the company holds an interest; or

(b) he or an associate of his must not control the company or possess more than 30 per cent of the ordinary share capital, or loan capital and issued share capital or voting power in the company.

For these purposes an associate includes a husband or wife, lineal ancestor or descendant, a partner and certain persons with whom the individual has connections through a trust.

"Paid director" means a director who receives remuneration. An unpaid director would not be disqualified merely because he was reimbursed travelling or other expenses allowable for tax purposes.

Tax relief

A qualifying individual can claim income tax relief on his investment in a qualifying company at his highest rate(s) of tax up to a total of £40,000 in any one tax year. Relief is not given for investments of less than £500 in any tax year where the claimant invests directly. This lower limit does not apply where the investment is made on his behalf by the managers of an approved investment fund.

The £40,000 limit applies equally to an individual and to a married couple. Relief will be given for the current tax year.

In the case of a fund relief will still be given in any year so long as 90 per cent of the total monies in the fund are invested within six months of the date of the fund closing.

One half of any investment at the election of the investor may be carried back to the previous tax year, with a carry back limit of £5,000 provided that the shares are issued prior to the 6th October in any year (extended to the 27th October in 1988 because of a postal strike).

The £40,000 limit referred to above includes any relief carried back from the first half of the following year.

There is a £5,000,000 ceiling on the total amount of relief that can be claimed in any year by all investors for investments in a company letting dwelling-houses on qualified assured tenancies. If the total exceeds the permitted maximum, no relief is given in respect of the excess.

Claim for relief

Claims for tax relief can be made when the qualifying activities have been carried on for at least four months. It must be made within two years of that date, or if later, two years from the end of the year of assessment in which the shares are issued.

Claims must be accompanied by Form BES1 issued by the company with the authority of its Inspector of Taxes to the effect that the company is a qualifying company carrying on qualifying activities.

The company then issues to the investor a tax relief certificate BES3. The claimant seeking relief must then submit the BES certificate to his or her own tax inspector. If the company later fails to carry on the stated activity relief could be withdrawn. Relief is reduced if during the first four years after the issue of eligible shares the company carries on its activities in partnership or joint venture with any other company.

Relief on loans

One operation involving a large number of companies that has attracted wide investment support has been brought to the market by William de Broe, the stockbrokers.

The object of the operation is to achieve a number of separate tax reductions.

These are: (a) the normal BES relief; (b) tax relief on interest paid by investors on "qualifying loans"; and (c) small companies relief.

As to (b), interest is tax deductible if it arises in connection with a qualifying loan which is made to an individual to enable him to acquire ordinary share capital of a close company. Under the operation investors are invited to apply for a loan in respect of the purchase price of a substantial part of the investment. Each company has nine investors with equal shareholding i.e. approximately 11 per cent.

The result is that no more than five investors control more than 50 per cent with the result that the company is a close one.

The borrower in these circumstances will have the necessary material interest in the company because he will have a beneficial interest of more than 5 per cent of the company. As to (c) if a company has profits of £100,000 or less in any accounting period then corporation tax is payable at 25 per cent and not at 35 per cent.

The success of the operation is of course dependent on the complete separation of one company from another in the Link scheme.

Tax avoidance

Relief is not available unless shares are subscribed and issued for bona fide commercial purposes and not as part of a scheme or arrangement, the main purpose, or one of the main purposes of which, is the avoidance of tax.

Withdrawal of relief

If the conditions of the relief relating to the company itself cease to be satisfied within four years of the shares being issued the relief is withdrawn.

Relief will be wholly or partly withdrawn if the investor receives value from the company or disposes of the shares within five years of the issue of the shares.

Examples of value received from the company are redemption of the shares, a loan to the investor or the provision of a benefit or facility.

If the shares are disposed of within the five year period then relief is withdrawn in full if the disposal is not at arm's length. But if it is then the relief is withdrawn up to the amount of the sale proceeds.

The receipt of a bona fide dividend will be excluded.

Relief is not lost where the claimant disposes of the shares to a spouse living with the claimant.

Capital gains tax

Qualifying shares are exempt from capital gains tax on their first disposal after more than five years from the date of issue unless at any time up to the date of disposal the business expansion scheme relief has been wholly withdrawn.

Even if part of the business expansion scheme relief has been withdrawn the whole of the investment is still exempt from capital gains tax.

Funds

Whereas a qualifying company may only raise £5,000,000 an approved investment fund is unlimited in the amount which it may raise so long as not more than £5,000,000 is invested by it in any single company.

Death of a participant

So long as the circumstances are such that immediately before the death of a participant he was entitled to tax relief, his death is not an occurrence which gives rise to the withdrawal of that relief.

There may, however, be practical difficulties in repaying the amount invested. In the ordinary way monies uninvested at death should be repaid to the estate. Disposal of issued shares may well present difficulties. Those entitled on death may well be wise to await until such time as the shares become marketable.

Chapter 14

Nature of a BES Tenancy

Because of the wish to have a valuable realisable asset at the end of five years after the issue of shares many of the BES companies have indicated the kind of tenants they will be seeking.

An element present in some but by no means all is mobility that is to say after a few years the tenant will have moved elsewhere.

The description of the tenants that are being sought include the staff and students at universities, teaching hospitals, colleges of further education, arts and technology, language schools, newly qualified and trainee professionals, newly married couples, single or divorced persons. Some companies intend to operate in a locality with high technological or specialist activities e.g. near to the North Sea oil rigs. Whether all the proposed tenants would in fact occupy the dwelling-houses as their only or principal homes will have to be determined, it would seem, in accordance with the tests laid down in *Hampstead Way Investments Ltd.* v. *Lewis-Weare* 274 Estates Gazette 281 [1985] 1 WLR 164.

Somewhat more surprisingly a number of companies have targeted the elderly. In the light of the provisions of section 17 it may be, although the prospectuses do not say so, that only single persons will be sought. What is clear either expressly or implicitly is that manual workers and persons with a child or children will not ordinarily be sought as tenants.

Good management in the selection of tenants will obviously be essential.

In some cases premises will be converted into flats; in other cases premises in disrepair will be brought into a habitable state. Most lettings will be unfurnished but a few will be furnished.

A periodic tenancy may prove to have attractive features for a BES company. Although by a late amendment of section 5(1) a landlord's notice to quit is ineffective, his right to bring the tenancy to an end, if he has an available ground for possession, is protected by section 8(4)(b).

If a tenant serves a notice to quit it ceases to be an assured tenancy so that section 7 does not apply. If the tenant does not vacate on due date the landlord has an immediate right to possession which he can enforce in the courts without reference to the 1988 Act.

The initial rent will be an open market one. BES tenancies are likely to contain provisions for rent increases. Landlords will seek to agree with tenants for increases based on some index such as the Retail Price or wages with or without some additional percentage. Rent review provisions dependent on arbitration are not likely to be a preferred method.

A flip-flop or pendulum valuation under which the valuer determines which of the proposals put forward by the landlord and tenant respectively is to be the new rent is another alternative method.

The advantage to a landlord of a periodic tenancy containing rent review provisions is that there will never be a reference to a rent assessment committee.

In the case, however, of a periodic tenancy which contains no rent review provisions or on the ending of a fixed term tenancy the landlord is entitled in the circumstances set out in the 1988 Act to seek an increase of rent from a rent assessment committee.

The BES tenancy may well have an absolute covenant against assignment.

Chapter 15

Realisation by BES Investors

In the case of BES companies the shares will ordinarily be held by the investor. In the case of Funds ordinarily the managers will transfer the shares to an investor at the end of the five year period. A number of Fund managers, however, appreciating the problems that may arise immediately at the end of the five year period are reserving to themselves the right to hold shares for an additional period of up to 2 years. However investors are likely to be concerned to realise their investments five years after they were issued their shares. This in practice is likely to present problems for BES companies and Fund managers.

The most commonly indicated alternatives are:

(1) Seeking a quotation on the Stock Exchange or on the unlisted securities market or third market.

(2) An offer by an identified or unidentified third party for the whole issued share capital either in cash or marketable shares.

(3) A matched bargain sale and purchase of a particular investor's shares whilst the company continued to operate.

(4) The purchase of shares by the company itself under the provisions of section 162 of the Companies Act 1985 subject to individual shareholders agreement and the appropriate corporate and Inland Revenue approvals.

(5) The liquidation of the company and the distribution of its funds in the winding up or reduction of capital pursuant to the order of the High Court.

Where the company is able to realise its assets in an advantageous way e.g. by the sale of the dwelling-house with vacant possession either (4) or (5) will be the likely exit route.

Where, however, that cannot be achieved or can only be achieved by a limited extent the most advantageous exit route for an investor will be (2). Whilst Fund managers may regard this as a desirable approach some BES company boards may not.

Whether the expense of a full Stock Exchange quotation would be economically justified must be doubtful. Obtaining a USM quotation is not cheap. In many USM shares the spread between buying and selling prices is proving unsatisfactory. The third market at the time of the publication of this book has not proved a significant success. It was hoped to provide an exit route for many non assured tenancy BES companies. Time will tell whether this market achieves that purpose. Whilst the sale of shares would not be subject for a qualifying investor to capital gains tax the company itself may be liable on the sale of its assets if course (4) is followed. It may well be tax effective for the sales of properties to take place over a number of years. The value of the house may of course not continue to rise or at least not continue to rise at anything like the rate of recent years. In practice tenants may not prove as mobile as had been expected. This particularly could happen if there was an economic recession. Sales to sitting tenants could result in a BES company having to accept prices substantially lower than the vacant possession value of the dwelling-house.

The elderly are unlikely to be keen buyers of the freehold: indeed an elderly person may have already sold a freehold dwelling-house prior to becoming a tenant. Unless a sale to a third party or a one hundred per cent sale of assets is achieved management expenses may erode the income; indeed they may exceed the income.

Some prospectuses contain complex provisions relating to the realisation of assets by investors particularly so far as incentives for a management company are concerned.

APPENDICES

A—Prescribed Notices

B—Section 39(1) of the 1988 Act

C—Section 4 of the 1976 Act

S.I. 1988 No. 2203

LANDLORD AND TENANT, ENGLAND AND WALES

The Assured Tenancies and Agricultural Occupancies (Forms) Regulations 1988

Made - - - -	*14th December 1988*
Coming into force	*15th January 1989*

The Secretary of State for the Environment, as respects England, and the Secretary of State for Wales, as respects Wales, in exercise of the powers conferred upon them by sections 6(2) and (3), 8(3), 13(2) and (4), 20(2), 22(1), 41(2) and 45(1) and (5) of the Housing Act 1988**(a)**, and of all other powers enabling them in that behalf, hereby make the following Regulations:

1. These Regulations may be cited as the Assured Tenancies and Agricultural Occupancies (Forms) Regulations 1988 and shall come into force on 15th January 1989.

2. In these Regulations any reference to a section is to a section of the Housing Act 1988 and any reference to a numbered form is a reference to the form bearing that number in the Schedule to these Regulations, or to a form substantially to the same effect.

3. The forms prescribed for the purposes of Part I of the Housing Act 1988 shall be as follows–

(1) for a notice under section 6(2) proposing terms of a statutory periodic tenancy different from the implied terms, form no. 1;

(2) for an application under section 6(3) referring a notice under section 6(2) to a rent assessment committee, form no. 2;

(3) for a notice under section 8 informing a tenant that the landlord intends to begin proceedings for possession of a dwelling-house let on an assured tenancy which is not an assured agricultural occupancy, form no. 3;

(4) for a notice under section 8 informing a tenant that the landlord intends to begin proceedings for possession of a dwelling-house let on an assured agricultural occupancy, form no. 4;

(5) for a notice under section 13(2) proposing a new rent for an assured tenancy which is not an assured agricultural occupancy, form no. 5;

(6) for an application under section 13(4) referring to a rent assessment committee a notice under section 13(2) relating to an assured tenancy or an assured agricultural occupancy, form no. 6;

(7) for a notice under section 20 of intention to grant an assured shorthold tenancy, form no. 7;

(8) for an application under section 22(1) to a rent assessment committee for a determination of rent under an assured shorthold tenancy, form no. 8; and

---

(a) 1988 c.50; in section 45(1), *see* the definition of "prescribed".

(9) for a notice under section 41(2) requiring a landlord or tenant to give information to a rent assessment committee, form no. 9.

Signed by authority of the Secretary of State
13th December 1988

John Selwyn Gummer
Minister of State,
Department of the Environment

14th December 1988

Peter Walker
Secretary of State for Wales

SCHEDULE

FORM No. 1

Housing Act 1988 section 6(2)

Notice Proposing Different Terms for Statutory Periodic Tenancy

- Please write clearly in black ink.
- **This notice proposes changes to the terms of the statutory periodic tenancy. If you wish to refer it to a rent assessment committee you must keep to the time limit set out in paragraph 2 below.**
- Please read this notice very carefully as it may alter the terms of the statutory periodic tenancy which arises when a fixed term assured tenancy runs out. It may also be used when a fixed term assured agricultural occupancy ends.
- It can be used by either a landlord or a tenant.

- This notice must be served no later than the first anniversary of the day after the former fixed term tenancy or occupancy ended.
- Do not use this notice if you are a landlord only proposing an increase in rent.
- If you need help or advice about this notice, and what you should do about it, take it immediately to any of the following:
  - a Citizens' Advice Bureau
  - a housing aid centre,
  - a law centre or a solicitor.

1. To:

Name(s) of landlord(s) or tenant(s)*

of:

Address of premises

2. This is to give notice that I/we* propose different terms of the statutory periodic tenancy from those in the fixed term assured tenancy which has now ended to take effect from

19

This date must be at least three months after this notice is served.

102

**Cross out whichever does not apply.*

- If you agree with the new terms and rent proposed, do nothing. They will become the terms of your tenancy agreement on the date specified in paragraph 2.
- If you don't agree with the proposed terms and any adjustment of the rent (see paragraph 4), and you are unable to reach agreement with your landlord/tenant, or you do not wish to discuss it with him, you may refer the matter directly to your local rent assessment committee, **within three months of the date on which the notice was served,** using a special form.
- The committee will determine the proposed changes in the terms of the tenancy or some other different terms covering the same points, and the appropriate level of rent, if this applies.

3. Changes to the terms

    (a)   The provisions of the tenancy to be changed are–
            Please attach relevant sections of the agreement if available.

    (b)   The proposed changes are–
             (*Continue on a separate sheet if necessary.*)

4.*Changes to the rent, if applicable

The existing rent is
This includes rates*

| £ | per |

eg. week, month, year

The new rent which takes into account
the proposed changes in the terms of the tenancy
will be–

| £ | per |

eg. week, month, year

This includes rates*

- Changes to the rent are optional. A proposal to adjust the rent to take account of the proposed new terms at paragraph 3 may be made if either the landlord or the tenant considers it appropriate.

To be signed by the landlord or his agent (someone acting for him) or the tenant or his agent. If there are joint landlords or joint tenants each landlord/tenant or the agent must sign unless one signs on behalf of the rest with their agreement.

Signed

*Name(s) of land-
lord(s)/tenant(s)*

*Address of land-
lord(s)/tenant(s)*

Tel:

If signed by agent, name and address of agent

Tel: *Date:*   19

Cross out if this does not apply.   103

Housing Act 1988 section 6(3)

Application Referring a Notice Under Section 6(2) to a Rent Assessment Committee

- Please write clearly in black ink.

- Please tick boxes where appropriate.

- When you have filled the form in please send it to the appropriate rent assessment panel.

- Make sure you also send a copy of the notice served on you proposing the new terms of the statutory periodic tenancy.

- This application may be used by a landlord or a tenant who has been served with a notice under section 6(2) of the Housing Act 1988, varying the terms of a statutory periodic tenancy. It may also be used where there was an earlier assured agricultural occupancy.

1. Address of premises

2. Name(s) of tenant(s)

3. Name(s) of landlord(s)

   Address of landlord(s)

4. Details of premises.

   (a) What type of property is it, eg house, flat or room(s)?

   (b) If it is a flat or room(s) say what floor(s) it is on.

   (c) Give the number and type of rooms, eg living room, bathroom.

   (d) Does the tenancy include any other facilities, eg garden, garage or other separate building or land?　　Yes ☐　　No ☐

   (e) If Yes, please give details.

   (f) Is any of the accommodation shared?
   　　(i) with the landlord?　　Yes ☐　　No ☐
   　　(ii) with another tenant or tenants?　　Yes ☐　　No ☐

   (g) If Yes, please give details.

5. What is the current rateable value of the premises?

£ _____

6. When did the statutory tenancy begin?

_____ 19 ____

7. Services

   (a) Are any services provided under the tenancy (eg cleaning, lighting, heating, hot water or gardening)?

      Yes ☐   No ☐

   (b) If Yes, please give details.

   (c) Is a separate charge made for services, maintenance, repairs, landlord's costs of management or any other item?

      Yes ☐   No ☐

   (d) What charge is payable?

      £ _____

   (e) Does the charge vary according to the relevant costs?

      Yes ☐   No ☐

   (f) If Yes, please give details.

8. (a) Is any furniture provided under the tenancy?

      Yes ☐   No ☐

   (b) If Yes, please give details (*continue on a separate sheet if necessary*).

9. What repairs are the responsibility of

   (a) the landlord?

   (b) the tenant? (*continue on a separate sheet if necessary*).

10. (a) Give details of the other terms of the tenancy, eg whether the tenancy is assignable and whether a premium may be charged on an assignment (*continue on a separate sheet if necessary*).

   (b) Please attach the tenancy agreement (or a copy), with a note of any variations, if you have one. It will be returned to you without delay.

11. I/We* attach a copy of the notice proposing changes to the statutory periodic tenancy and, if applicable, an adjustment of the amount of rent and apply to the rent assessment committee to consider it.

Cross out whichever does not apply.

To be signed by the landlord or his agent (someone acting for him), or by the tenant or his agent. If there are joint landlords or joint tenants each landlord/tenant or the agent must sign, unless one signs on behalf of the rest with their agreement.

Signed

Name(s) of land-lord(s)/tenant(s)

Address of land-lord(s)/tenant(s)

Tel:

If signed by agent, name and address of agent

Tel: *Date:*   19

FORM No. 3

Housing Act 1988 section 8

Notice Seeking Possession of a Property
Let on an Assured Tenancy

- Please write clearly in black ink.

- Do not use this form if possession is sought from an assured shorthold tenant under section 21 of the Housing Act 1988 or if the property is occupied under an assured agricultural occupancy.

- **This notice is the first step towards requiring you to give up possession of your home. You should read it very carefully.**

- If you need advice about this notice, and what you should do about it, take it as quickly as possible to any of the following–
  - a Citizens' Advice Bureau,
  - a housing aid centre,
  - a law centre,
  - or a solicitor.

  You may be able to get Legal Aid but this will depend on your personal circumstances.

1. To: [   ]   *Name(s) of tenant(s)*

2. Your landlord intends to apply to the court for an order requiring you to give up possession of–

[   ]   *Address of premises*

- If you have an assured tenancy under the Housing Act 1988, which is not an assured shorthold tenancy, you can only be required to leave your home if your landlord gets an order for possession from the court on one of the grounds which are set out in Schedule 2 to the Act.

- If you are willing to give up possession of your home without a court order, you should tell the person who signed this notice as soon as possible and say when you can leave.

3. The landlord intends to seek possession on ground(s) [   ] **in Schedule 2 to the Housing Act 1988, which reads**

Give the full text of each ground which is being relied on. (Continue on a separate sheet if necessary.)

[   ]

- Whichever grounds are set out in paragraph 3 the court may allow any of the other grounds to be added at a later date. If this is done, you will be told about it so you can discuss the additional grounds at the court hearing as well as the grounds set out in paragraph 3.

4. Particulars of each ground are as follows–

Give a full explanation of why each ground is being relied. (Continue on a separate sheet if necessary.)

[   ]

- If the court is satisfied that any of grounds 1 to 8 is established it must make an order (but see below in respect of fixed term tenancies).

- Before the court will grant an order on any of grounds 9 to 16, it must be satisfied that it is reasonable to require you to leave. This means that, if one of these grounds is set out in paragraph 3, you will be able to suggest to the court that it is not reasonable that you should have to leave, even if you accept that the ground applies.

- The court will not make an order under grounds 1, 3 to 7, 9 or 16, to take effect during the fixed term of the tenancy; and it will only make an order during the fixed term on grounds 2, 8 or 10 to 15 if the terms of the tenancy make provision for it to be brought to an end on any of these grounds.

107

- Where the court makes an order for possession solely on ground 6 or 9, your landlord or licensor must pay your reasonable removal expenses.

5. The court proceedings will not begin until after

	19

Give the date after which court proceedings can be brought.

- Where the landlord or licensor is seeking possession under grounds 1, 2, 5 to 7 or 9 in Schedule 2, court proceedings cannot begin earlier than 2 months from the date this notice is served on you and not before the date on which the tenancy or licence (had it not been an assured agricultural occupancy) could have been brought to an end by a notice to quit or determine served at the same time as this notice.

- Where the landlord or licensor is seeking possession on grounds 3, 4, 8 or 10 to 15, court proceedings cannot begin until 2 weeks after the date this notice is served.

- After the date shown in paragraph 5, court proceedings may be begun at once but not later than 12 months from the date this notice is served. After this time the notice will lapse and a new notice must be served before possession can be sought.

To be signed by the landlord, the licensor or his agent (someone acting for him).

Signed

*Name(s) of
landlord(s)
or licensor(s)*

*Address of
landlord(s)
or licensor(s)*

Tel:

If signed by agent, name and address of agent

Tel: *Date:*   19

108

FORM No. 4

Housing Act 1988 section 8

Notice Seeking Possession of an
Assured Agricultural Occupancy

- Please write clearly in black ink.
- **This notice is the first step towards requiring you to give up possession of your home. You should read it very carefully.**
- If you need advice about this notice, and what you should do about it, take it as quickly as possible to any of the following–

- a Citizens' Advice Bureau,
- a housing aid centre,
- a law centre,
- or a solicitor.

You may be able to get Legal Aid but this will depend on your personal circumstances.

1. To: [ ] *Name(s) of tenant(s) or licensee(s)*

2. **Your landlord or licensor intends to apply to the court for an order requiring you to give up possession of–**

   [ ] *Address of premises*

- If you have an assured agricultural occupancy under the Housing Act 1988, which is not an assured shorthold tenancy, you can only be required to leave your home if your landlord or licensor gets an order for possession from the court on one of the grounds which are set out in Schedule 2 to the Act, except ground 16.

- If you are willing to give up possession of your home without a court order, you should tell the person who signed this notice as soon as possible and say when you can leave.

3. **The landlord or licensor intends to seek possession on ground(s)** [ ] **in Schedule 2 to the Housing Act 1988, which reads**
   Give the full text of each ground which is being relied on. Continue on a separate sheet if necessary.)

   [ ]

- Whichever grounds are set out in paragraph 3 the court may allow any of the other grounds to be added at a later date. If this is done, you will be told about it so you can discuss the additional grounds at the court hearing as well as the grounds set out in paragraph 3.

4. **Particulars of each ground are as follows–**
   Give a full explanation of why each ground is being relied. (Continue on a separate sheet if necessary.)

   [ ]

- If the court is satisfied that any of grounds 1 to 8 is established it must make an order (but see below in respect of fixed term tenancies or licences).

- Before the court will grant an order on any of grounds 9 to 15, it must be satisfied that it is reasonable to require you to leave. This means that, if one of these grounds is set out in paragraph 3, you will be able to suggest to the court that it is not reasonable that you should have to leave, even if you accept that the ground applies.

- The court will not make an order under grounds 1, 3 to 7 or 9, to take effect during the fixed term of the tenancy or licence; and it will only make an order during the fixed term on grounds 2, 8 or 10 to 15 if the terms of the tenancy or licence make provision for it to be brought to an end on any of these grounds.

- Where the court makes an order for possession solely on ground 6 or 9, your landlord must pay your reasonable removal expenses.

5. The court proceedings will not begin until after

	19

Give the date after which court proceedings can be brought.

- Where the landlord is seeking possession under grounds 1, 2, 5 to 7, 9 or 16 in Schedule 2, court proceedings cannot begin earlier than 2 months from the date this notice is served on you and not before the date on which the tenancy (had it not been assured) could have been brought to an end by a notice to quit served at the same time as this notice.

- Where the landlord is seeking possession on grounds 3, 4, 8 or 10 to 15, court proceedings cannot begin until 2 weeks after the date this notice is served.

- After the date shown in paragraph 5, court proceedings may be begun at once but not later than 12 months from the date this notice is served. After this time the notice will lapse and a new notice must be served before possession can be sought.

To be signed by the landlord or his agent (someone acting for him).

Signed

Name(s) of landlord(s)

Address of landlord(s)

Tel:

If signed by agent, name and address of agent

Tel: *Date:*   19

FORM No. 5

Housing Act 1988 section 13(2)

Landlord's Notice Proposing a New Rent Under An Assured Periodic Tenancy or Agricultural Occupancy

- Please write clearly in black ink.

- Do not use this form if there is a current rent fixing mechanism in the tenancy.

- Do not use this form to propose a rent adjustment for a statutory periodic tenancy solely because of a proposed change of terms under section 6(2) of the Housing Act 1988.

- This notice may also be used to propose a new rent or licence fee for an assured agricultural occupancy. In such a case references to "landlord"/"tenant" can be read as references to "licensor"/"licensee" etc.

- **This notice proposes a new rent. If you want to oppose this proposal you must keep to the time limit set out in paragraph 2.** Read this notice carefully. If you need help or advice take it immediately to:
  - a Citizens' Advice Bureau,
  - a housing aid centre,
  - a law centre,
  - or a solicitor.

1. To: _____ *Name(s) of tenant(s)*

   of: _____ *Address of premises*

   _____

   _____

2. This is to give notice that as from _____ 19____

   your landlord proposes to charge a new rent.

   The new rent must take effect at the beginning of a new period of the tenancy and not earlier than any of the following–

   (a) the minimum period after this notice was served,
   (The minimum period is–
   - in the case of a yearly tenancy, six months,
   - in the case of a tenancy where the period is less than a month, one month, and,
   - in any other case, a period equal to the period of the tenancy.)

   (b) the first anniversary of the start of the first period of the tenancy except in the case of–
   - a statutory periodic tenancy, which arises when a fixed term assured tenancy ends, or
   - an assured tenancy which arose on the death of a tenant under a regulated tenancy,

   (c) if the rent under the tenancy has previously been increased by a notice under section 13 or a determination under section 14 of the Housing Act 1988, the first anniversary of the date on which the increased rent took effect.

3. The existing rent is   £ _____ per _____

   eg. week, month, year

   This includes/excludes* rates

4. The proposed new rent will be   £ _____ per _____

   eg. week, month, year

   This includes/excludes* rates   111

Cross out whichever does not apply.

- If you agree with the new rent proposed do nothing. If you do not agree and you are unable to reach agreement with your landlord or do not want to discuss it directly with him, you may refer the notice to your local rent assessment committee before the beginning of the new period given in paragraph 2. The committee will consider your application and will decide whether the proposed new rent is appropriate.

- You will need a special form to refer the notice to a rent assessment committee.

To be signed by the landlord or his agent (someone acting for him). If there are joint landlords each landlord or his agent must sign unless one signs on behalf of the rest with their agreement.

Signed

Name(s) of
landlord(s)

Address of
landlord(s)

Tel:

If signed by agent, name and address of agent

Tel: Date: 19

112

Housing Act 1988 section 13(4)

Application Referring A Notice Proposing A New Rent Under An Assured Periodic Tenancy or Agricultural Occupancy to a Rent Assessment Committee

- Please write clearly in black ink.
- Please tick boxes where appropriate.
- When you have filled the form in please send it to the appropriate rent assessment panel.

- You should use this form when your landlord has served notice on you proposing a new rent under an assured periodic tenancy.
- You will need to attach a copy of that notice to this form.
- This form may also be used to refer a notice proposing a new rent or licence fee for an assured agricultural occupancy. In such a case references to "landlord"/ "tenant" can be read as references to "licensor"/"licensee" etc.

1. Address of premises

2. Name(s) of landlord(s)

   Address of landlord(s)

3. Details of premises.
   (a) What type of property is it, eg house, flat or room(s)?

   (b) If it is a flat or room(s) say what floor(s) it is on.

   (c) Give the number and type of rooms, eg living room, bathroom.

   (d) Does the tenancy include any other facilities, eg garden, garage or other separate building or land?   Yes ☐   No ☐

   (e) If Yes, please give details.

   (f) Do you share any accommodation?
       (i) with the landlord?   Yes ☐   No ☐
       (ii) with another tenant or tenants?   Yes ☐   No ☐

   (g) If Yes to either of the above, please give details.

113

4. What is the current rateable value of the premises?

£

5. (a) When did the present tenancy begin?

19

(b) When does the present tenancy end?

19

6. (a) Did you pay a premium?   Yes ☐   No ☐

(b) If Yes, please give details.

7. Services

(a) Are any services provided under the tenancy (eg cleaning, lighting, heating, hot water or gardening)?   Yes ☐   No ☐

(b) If Yes please give details.

(c) Is a separate charge made for services, maintenance, repairs, landlord's costs of management or any other item?   Yes ☐   No ☐

(d) What charge is payable?

£

(e) Does the charge vary according to the relevant costs?   Yes ☐   No ☐

(f) If Yes, please give details.

8. (a) Is any furniture provided under the tenancy?   Yes ☐   No ☐

(b) If Yes, please give details (*continue on a separate sheet if necessary*).

9. Improvements

(a) Have you, or any former tenant(s) carried out improvements or replaced fixtures, fittings or furniture for which you or they were not responsible under the terms of the tenancy?   Yes ☐   No ☐

(b) If Yes, please give details (*continue on a separate sheet if necessary*).

114

10. What repairs are the responsibility of

    (a) the landlord?

    (b) the tenant?
        (continue on a separate sheet if necessary).

11. (a) Give details of the other terms of the tenancy, eg whether the tenancy is assignable and whether a premium may be charged on an assignment
        (continue on a separate sheet if necessary).

    (b) Please attach the tenancy agreement, or a copy (with a note of any variations), if you have one. It will be returned to you as quickly as possible.

12. Do you have an assured agricultural occupancy?   Yes ☐   No ☐

13. I/We* attach a copy of the notice proposing a new rent under the assured periodic tenancy and I/we* apply for it to be considered by a rent assessment committee.

To be signed by the tenant or his agent (someone acting for him). If there are joint tenants, each tenant or his agent must sign, unless one signs on behalf of the rest with their agreement.

Signed	
Name of tenant(s)	
Address of tenant(s)	
Tel:	

If signed by agent, name and address of agent

Tel:		*Date:*	19

Cross out whichever does not apply.

115

Housing Act 1988 section 20

Notice of an Assured Shorthold Tenancy

- Please write clearly in black ink.

- If there is any thing you do not understand you should get advice from a solicitor or a Citizens' Advice Bureau, before you agree to the tenancy.

- The landlord must give this notice to the tenant before an assured shorthold tenancy is granted. It does not commit the tenant to take the tenancy.

- **This document is important, keep it in a safe place.**

To: [   ]

Name of proposed tenant. If a joint tenancy is being offered enter the names of the joint tenants.

1. *You are proposing to take a tenancy of the dwelling known as:*

[   ]

from [/ /19] to [/ /19]

  day month year   day month year

The tenancy must be for a term certain of at least six months.

2. This notice is to tell you that your tenancy is to be an assured shorthold tenancy. Provided you keep to the terms of the tenancy, you are entitled to remain in the dwelling for at least the first six months of the fixed period agreed at the start of the tenancy. At the end of this period, depending on the terms of the tenancy, the landlord may have the right to repossession if he wants.

3. The rent for this tenancy is the rent we have agreed. However, you have the right to apply to a rent assessment committee for a determination of the rent which the committee considers might reasonably be obtained under the tenancy. If the committee considers (i) that there is a sufficient number of similar properties in the locality let on assured tenancies and that (ii) the rent we have agreed is significantly higher than the rent which might reasonably be obtained having regard to the level of rents for other assured tenancies in the locality, it will determine a rent for the tenancy. That rent will be the legal maximum you can be required to pay from the date the committee directs.

4. This notice was served on you on [19]

To be signed by the landlord or his agent (someone acting for him). If there are joint landlords each must sign, unless one signs on behalf of the rest with their agreement.

Signed	[ ]
Name(s) of landlord(s)	[ ]
Address of landlord(s)	[ ]
Tel:	[ ]

If signed by agent, name and address of agent

Tel: | *Date:* 19

Special note for existing tenants

- Generally if you already have a protected or statutory tenancy and you give it up to take a new tenancy in the same or other accommodation owned by the same landlord, that tenancy cannot be an assured tenancy. It can still be a protected tenancy.

- But if you currently occupy a dwelling which was let to you as a protected shorthold tenant, special rules apply.

- If you have an assured tenancy which is not a shorthold under the Housing Act 1988, you cannot be offered an assured shorthold tenancy of the same or other accommodation by the same landlord.

FORM No. 8

Housing Act 1988 section 22(1)

Application to a Rent Assessment Committee for a Determination of a Rent Under an Assured Shorthold Tenancy

- Please write clearly in black ink.

- Please tick boxes where appropriate.

- A tenant with a fixed term assured shorthold tenancy may use this form to apply to the local rent assessment committee, during the fixed term, to have the rent reduced. This form cannot be used in the cases specified at the end of this form.

- The form may also be used to apply to have the rent reduced for a fixed term assured shorthold tenancy which is an assured agricultural occupancy. In such a case, references to "landlord"/"tenant" can be read as references to "licensor"/ "licensee" etc.

- When you have filled the form in please send it to the appropriate rent assessment panel.

1. Address of premises

2. Name(s) of landlord(s)

   Address of landlord(s)

3. Details of premises.
   - (a) What type of property is it, eg house, flat or room(s)?
   - (b) If it is a flat or room(s) say what floor(s) it is on.
   - (c) Give the number and type of rooms, eg living room, bathroom etc.
   - (d) Does the tenancy include any other facilities, eg garden, garage or other separate building or land?   Yes ☐   No ☐
   - (e) If Yes, please give details.

   - (f) Do you share any accommodation?
     - (i) with the landlord?   Yes ☐   No ☐
     - (ii) with another tenant or tenants?   Yes ☐   No ☐
   - (g) If Yes to either of the above, please give details.

4. What is the current rateable value of the premises?   £

118

5. (a) When did the present tenancy begin?

[19   ]

(b) When does the present tenancy end?

[   ]

6. (a) Please confirm by ticking box that you received a notice saying that the tenancy ☐
   was to be an assured shorthold tenancy before the agreement was entered into.

   (b) Attach a copy of the notice if available.
       It will be returned without delay.

7. (a) Did you pay a premium?   Yes ☐   No ☐

   (b) If Yes, please give details.

[   ]
[   ]
[   ]

8. Services

   (a) Are any services provided under the tenancy   Yes ☐   No ☐
       (eg cleaning, lighting, heating, hot water or
       gardening)?

   (b) If Yes, please give details.

[   ]
[   ]
[   ]

   (c) Is a separate charge made for services,   Yes ☐   No ☐
       maintenance, repairs, landlord's costs of
       management or any other item?

   (d) What charge is payable?   [£   ]

   (e) Does the charge vary according to the   Yes ☐   No ☐
       relevant costs?

   (f) If Yes, please give details.

[   ]
[   ]
[   ]

9. (a) Is any furniture provided under the tenancy?   Yes ☐   No ☐

   (b) If Yes, please give details
       (continue on a separate sheet if necessary).

[   ]
[   ]
[   ]

10. What repairs are the responsibility of

    (a) the landlord?

[   ]
[   ]

    (b) the tenant?
        (continue on a separate sheet if necessary).

[   ]

119

11. (a) Give details of the other terms of the tenancy, eg whether the tenancy is assignable, and whether a premium may be charged on an assignment
(*continue on a separate sheet if necessary*).

(b) Please attach the tenancy agreement or a copy (with a note of any variations) if you have one. It will be returned to you without delay.

12. The existing rent is

£   per

eg. week, month, year

This includes/excludes*   rates of

£   per

13 I/We* apply to the rent assessment committee to determine a rent for the above mentioned premises.

To be signed by the tenant or his agent (someone acting for him). If there are joint tenants each tenant or his agent must sign, unless one signs on behalf of the rest with their agreement.

Signed

Name(s) of tenant(s)

Address of tenant(s)

Tel:

If signed by agent, name and address of agent

Tel: Date: 19

- An application cannot be made if–
  - (a) the rent payable under the tenancy is a rent previously determined by a rent assessment committee; or
  - (b) the tenancy is an assured shorthold tenancy that came into being on the ending of a tenancy which had been an assured shorthold of the same, or substantially the same, property and the landlord and tenant under each tenancy were the same at that time.

- The rent assessment committee cannot make a determination unless it considers–
  - (a) that there is a sufficient number of similar dwelling-houses in the locality let on assured tenancies (whether shorthold or not); and
  - (b) that the rent payable under the shorthold tenancy in question is significantly higher than the rent which the landlord might reasonably be expected to get in comparison with other rents under the assured tenancies mentioned in (a) above.

Cross out whichever does not apply.

120

Housing Act 1988 section 41(2)

Notice by Rent Assessment Committee
Requiring Further Information

To: [_____] *Landlord(s)/tenant(s)**

of: [_____] *Address of premises*

[_____]

[_____]

1. An application has been made to the rent assessment committee for consideration of–
   * the terms of a statutory periodic assured tenancy
   * an increase in rent under an assured periodic tenancy
   * the rent under an assured shorthold tenancy
   * an increase in rent under an assured agricultural occupancy

   of the above property. The committee needs more information from you, to consider the application.

2. The information needed is

Please send it to

no later than [19]

3. If you fail to comply with this notice without reasonable cause you will be committing a criminal offence and may be liable to a fine.

Signed [_____] Date [19]

for the rent assessment committee

*Cross out whichever does not apply.

EXPLANATORY NOTE

(This note is not part of the Regulations)

These Regulations prescribe the forms to be used for the purposes of various provisions of Part I of the Housing Act 1988 relating to assured tenancies and assured agricultural occupancies.

1977 Act as amended by section 39(1) of the 1988 Act

Statutory tenants and tenancies

2(1) Subject to this Part of this Act:

(a) After the termination of a protected tenancy of a dwelling-house the person who, immediately before that termination, was the protected tenant of the dwelling-house shall if and so long as he occupies the dwelling-house as his residence, be the statutory tenant of it; and

(b) Part I of Schedule I to this Act shall have effect for determining what period (if any) is the statutory tenant of a dwelling-house *or as the case may be, is entitled to an assured tenancy of a dwelling-house by succession* at any time after the death of a person who immediately before his death, was either a protected tenant of the dwelling-house or the statutory tenant of it by virtue of paragraph (a) above.

Part I of Schedule 1 to the 1977 Act
as amended by section 39(2) and (3) of Schedule 4 to the
1988 Act

1. Paragraph 2 below shall have effect subject to Section 2 (3) of this Act, for the purpose of determining who is the statutory tenant of a dwelling-house by succession after the death of the person (in this part of the Schedule referred to as "the original tenant") who, immediately before his death, was a protected tenant of the dwelling-house or the statutory tenant of it by virtue of his previous protected tenancy.

2. (1) The surviving spouse (if any) of the original tenant, if residing in the dwelling-house immediately before the death of the original tenant, shall after the death be the statutory tenant if and so long as he or she occupies the dwelling-house as his residence.

(2) *For the purposes of this paragraph, a person who was living with the original tenant as his or her wife or husband shall be treated as the spouse of the original tenant.*

(3) *If immediately after the death of the original tenant, there is, by virtue of sub-paragraph (2) above, more than one person who fulfils the conditions in sub-paragraph (1) above, such one of them as may be decided by agreement or, in default of agreement,*

by the county court shall be treated as the surviving spouse for the purposes of this paragraph.

3. (1) Where paragraph 2 above does not apply but a person who was a member of the original tenant's family was residing with him *in the dwelling-house* at the time of and for the period of *two years* immediately before his death then, after his death that person or if there is more than one such person such one of them as may be decided by agreement, or in default of agreement by the county court, shall be *entitled to an assured tenancy of the dwelling-house by succession; and*

(2) *If the original tenant died within the period of 18 months beginning on the operative date, then, for the purposes of this paragraph, a person who was residing in the dwelling-house with the original tenant at the time of his death and for the period which began 6 months before the operative date and ended at the time of his death shall be taken to have been residing with the original tenant for the period of 2 years immediately before his death.*

4. A person who becomes the statutory tenant by virtue of paragraph 2 above is in this part of this Schedule referred to as "the first successor".

5. If, immediately before his death, the first successor was still a statutory tenant, paragraph 6 *below shall have effect* for the purpose of determining who is the statutory tenant after the death of the first successor.

6. *(1) Where a person who:*

  (a) *was a member of the original tenant's family immediately before that tenant's death, and*

  (b) *was a member of the first successor's family immediately before the first successor's death,*

was residing in the dwelling-house with the first successor at the time of, and for the period of 2 years immediately before, the first successor's death, that person or, if there is more than one such person, such one of them as may be decided by agreement or, in default of agreement, by the county court shall be entitled to an assured tenancy of the dwelling-house by succession.

(2) *If the first successor died within the period of 18 months beginning on the operative date, then, for the purposes of this paragraph, a person who was residing in the dwelling-house with the first successor at the time of his death and for the period which began 6 months before the operative date and ended at the time of his death shall be taken to have been residing with the first successor for the period of 2 years immediately before his death.*

9. Paragraphs 5 and 6 above do not apply where the statutory tenancy of the original tenant arose by virtue of section 4 of the

Requisition Houses and Housing (Amendment) Act 1955 or section 20 of the Rent Act 1965.

10. (1) Where after a succession the successor becomes the tenant of the dwelling-house by the grant to him of another tenancy, "the original tenant" and "the first successor" in this Part of this Schedule shall, in relation to that other tenancy, mean the persons who were respectively the original tenant and the first successor at the time of the succession, and accordingly:

(a) If the successor was the first successor, and, immediately before his death he was still the tenant (whether protected or statutory), paragraph 6 above shall apply on his death,

(b) if the successor was not the first successor, no person shall become a statutory tenant on his death by virtue of this Part of this Schedule.

(2) Sub-paragraph (1) above applies:

(a) even if a successor enters into more than one other tenancy of the dwelling-house, and

(b) even if both the first successor and the successor on his death enter into other tenancies of the dwelling-house.

(3) In this paragraph "succession" means the occasion on which a person becomes the statutory tenant of the dwelling-house by virtue of this Part of this Schedule and "successor" shall be construed accordingly.

(4) This paragraph shall apply as respects a succession which took place before 27th August 1972 if, and only if, the tenancy granted after the succession, or the first of those tenancies, was granted on or after that date, and where it does not apply as respects a succession, no account shall be taken of that succession in applying this paragraph as respects any later succession.

11. (1) Paragraphs 5 and 6 do not apply where:

(a) the tenancy of the original tenant was granted on or after the operative date within the meaning of the Rent (Agriculture) Act 1976, and

(b) both that tenancy and the statutory tenancy of the first successor were tenancies to which section 99 of this Act applies.

(2) if the tenants under both the tenancies falling within sub-paragraph (2) (b) were persons to whom paragraph 7 of Schedule 9 to the Rent (Agriculture) Act 1976 applies, the reference in sub-paragraph (2) (a) above to the operative date shall be taken as a reference to the date of operation for forestry workers within the meaning of that Act.

11A. *In this part of this Schedule "the operative date" means the date on which Part I of the Housing Act 1988 came into force.*

Appendix C

Section 4 of the 1976 Act
as amended by section 39(4)

Statutory tenants and tenancies

"4 (1) Subject to section 5 below, where a person ceases to be a protected occupier of a dwelling-house on the termination, whether by notice to quit or by virtue of Section 16 (3) of this Act or otherwise, of his licence or tenancy, he shall, if and so long as he occupies the dwelling-house as his residence, be the statutory tenant of it.

(2) Subject to section 5 below, subsection (3) below shall have effect for determining what person (if any) is the statutory tenant of a dwelling-house at any time after the death of a person ("the original occupier") who was, immediately before his death, a protected occupier or statutory tenant of the dwelling-house in his own right.

(3) If the original occupier was a man who died leaving a widow who was residing in the dwelling-house immediately before his death then after his death, unless the widow is a protected occupier of the dwelling-house by virtue of section 3 (2) above, she shall be the statutory tenant if and so long as she occupies the dwelling-house as her residence.

(4) Where:
   (a) the original occupier was not a person who died leaving a surviving spouse who was residing in the dwelling-house immediately before his death, but
   (b) one or more persons who were members of his family were residing with him *in the dwelling-house* at the time of and for the period of *two years* immediately before his death, then, after this death, unless that person or, as the case may be, one of those persons is a protected occupier of the dwelling-house by virtue of section 3 (3) above, that person or, as the case may be, such one of those persons as may be decided by agreement, or in the default of agreement by the county court, shall be *entitled to an assured tenancy of the dwelling-house by succession.*

(5) In subsections *(1) and (3)* above the phrase "if and so long

as he occupies the dwelling-house as his residence" shall be construed in accordance with section 2 (3) of the Rent Act 1977.

(5A) For the purposes of subsection (3) above, a person who was living with the original occupier as his or her wife or husband shall be treated as the spouse of the original occupier and subject to subsection (5B) below, the references in subsection (3) above to a widow and in subsection (4) above to a surviving spouse shall be construed accordingly.

(5B) If, immediately after the death of the original occupier there is by virtue of subsection (5A) above, more than one person who fulfils the conditions in subsection (3) above, such one of them as may be decided by agreement or, in default of agreement by the county court, shall be the statutory tenant by virtue of that subsection.

(5C) If the original occupier died within the period of 18 months beginning on the operative date, then, for the purposes of subsection (3) above, a person who was residing in the dwelling-house with the original occupier at the time of his death and for the period which began 6 months before the operative date and ended at the time of his death shall be taken to have been residing with the original occupier for the period of 2 years immediately before his death and in this subsection "the operative date" means the date on which Part I of the Housing Act 1988 came into force".

(6) A dwelling-house is, in this Act, referred to as subject to a statutory tenancy where there is a statutory tenant of it.

Index

A

B

R

S

T